ethics
and
twentieth century
thought

context of thought

edited by HARRY FRANKFURT

ethics and twentieth century thought FREDERICK A. OLAFSON

FREDERICK A. OLAFSON
University of California, San Diego

"ethics
and
twentieth century
thought"

170

Prentice-Hall, Inc., Englewood Cliffs, New Jersey

P-H [c1973]

Library of Congress Cataloging in Publication Data

Olafson, Frederick A.
  Ethics and Twentieth Century Thought.

  (Context of Thought)
  Bibliography: p.
  1. Ethics. 2. Social sciences and ethics.
I. Title II. Series.
BJ37.034   170   72–8962
ISBN 0-13-290528-0
ISBN 0-13-290510-8 (pbk)

For Peter, Christopher, and Thomas

Printed in the United States of America.

10 9 8 7 6 5 4 3 2 1

Prentice-Hall International, Inc., London
Prentice-Hall of Australia, Pty. Ltd., Sydney
Prentice-Hall of Canada, Ltd., Toronto
Prentice-Hall of India Private Limited, New Delhi
Prentice-Hall of Japan, Inc., Tokyo

contents

I   *ethics and philosophy*   *1*

II   *ethics and the social
     sciences*   *38*

III *ethics and the humanities*   *86*

introduction

There seems to be widespread agreement that in the course of the
twentieth century the situation of ethics considered as a form of judgment and of knowledge has become problematic in a way that is probably unprecedented. At the same time as the religious and metaphysical
systems of belief with which ethical doctrines have traditionally been
associated, have lost ground, the natural sciences which pride themselves
on their "value-neutrality" have celebrated great advances. The result
has been to leave ethical thought in an isolated position and to raise in
acute form questions about "the place of value in a world of fact." By
some this crisis of confidence in the substantiality of ethical distinctions
is held to be one of the reasons for what these same observers regard
as a decline in public morals. Others, like Professor Michael Polanyi,
diagnose our condition as a state of "moral inversion" in which a
strongly moral form of motivation is paired with a failure to acknowledge the existence of a distinctively moral component in human personality and judgment. What is certain is that with the eclipse of

teleological conceptions of nature and the world-process generally, we are no longer sure that we know how to integrate ethical phenomena and the ethical point of view into our system of the world.

The concern of this book is not with this set of issues as a whole, but rather with the ways in which a number of scholarly disciplines and one art—that of literature—have tried to come to terms with them. In general, their tendency has been to move toward an interpretation of their respective cognitive enterprises according to which a greater degree of scientific objectivity requires a substantial abandonment for the purposes of such study of any distinctively moral perspective upon the matters with which they deal. Of late, this movement toward objectivity has been severely condemned, largely on the grounds that the kind of self-objectification of scientific inquiry which it seeks to carry out is both philosophically invalid and socially pernicious. There have also been a number of recent attempts to reformulate our conceptions of knowledge and inquiry in such a way as to assign an essential place to "subjective" and evaluative considerations; but there does not yet appear to be any widely accepted reformulation of the epistemology of the various disciplines that would replace the old dichotomies of fact and value. Indeed, one may justifiably feel that the alternatives that are being offered merely replace an uncritical objectivism with an extreme and unregulated form of subjectivism.

The aims of this book in relation to this continuing controversy are modest; and it is primarily addressed to the student who needs some preliminary orientation within a complex discussion which has been going on throughout this century. Accordingly, I have undertaken to examine with some care the ways in which a number of major disciplines have tried to characterize ethical phenomena and to relate them to their own distinctive cognitive undertakings. No claim is made to anything like completeness of coverage even within the disciplines discussed; and whole disciplines that have an important bearing on these matters—evolutionary biology, for example—have been omitted. In general, my concern has been not so much with the ethical issues that arise in connection with the social applications of the various branches of knowledge as with the role of evaluative and moral judgments *within* the cognitive undertakings of these disciplines. While I do not think that my review of developments in these disciplines confirms in any straightforward way any of the rather partisan hypotheses I referred to at the outset, I have not been afraid to reach conclusions about many of the movements of thought I consider. It does not seem to me, however, that the motivating grounds for the movement toward objectivity and value-neutrality have been the same in all cases; and the very variety of the considerations that have motivated that movement make a nuanced and carefully modulated judgment necessary.

The disciplines with which I deal are philosophy, the social sciences, and the humanities. In each case my mode of treatment has been to follow a roughly chronological order and to take up first those ways of interpreting the ethical dimensions of a discipline which were widely accepted in the earlier years of the century. In the case of philosophy, this early stage was that of idealism in which typically a very close union of factual and evaluative, as well as of individual and social, forms of experience was insisted upon and the guiding role of ideas— moral ideas among them—was assumed as a matter of course. Analogues to the kind of synthesis that idealism represented in the case of philosophy can be found in the social sciences and the humanities as well; and there, as in my discussion of philosophy, I have tried to understand the later evolution of these disciplines, in the course of which the place of ethical ideas became more and more problematic, by first characterizing in some detail the "orthodox" position in these matters which, as I have suggested, tended to be the one most widely accepted at the beginning of the century. In some cases it is also possible to discern a tendency for views that enjoyed this kind of acceptance to be revived later in a significantly modified form; but in general the movement in most disciplines has not turned upon itself in this way. It is my hope that readers of this book will be led to explore for themselves the literature with which it deals. In so doing, they stand to gain a deeper sense of the complexity and concreteness of ethical thought and a better understanding of its broader human implications.

ONE

ethics and philosophy

*I*n one of its principal uses, the term "ethics" is the name of a subdivision of philosophy. Its scope is subject to differing interpretations, and it is sometimes understood to include everything that has to do with value and evaluative experience—everything, in the words of Ludwig Wittgenstein, that gives meaning to life. In this very broad interpretation, ethics comprises investigations into the generic meaning of "good" as well as its principal subvarieties such as aesthetic good and functional good. Usually, however, ethics is assumed to have a special interest in those values that have a bearing on human action and propose a goal for human effort; it is natural, therefore, that questions about the *summum bonum*—the good for man—should be of primary importance for ethical thought. But beyond the question of what is good there must arise the further question of what is right, and it is to this question about the consideration we must give to the interests of other human beings as we pursue our own good that ethics in the most familiar sense of the term addresses itself. Here ethics becomes an inquiry into the conditions that must be satisfied if one person's action is to be justifiable to another individual who may be significantly affected by it. The central concept for ethics in this sense is that of justice; and the central problem is whether the requirements of justice are compatible with the aspiration of each individual to achieve a state of happiness or well-being. All of these conceptions of ethics are, of course, perfectly legitimate; they are in fact closely related to one another at various points. In what follows, I will have occasion to deal with views that are ethical in all of these senses, but my main interest will be directed to views that in one way or another bear on ethics considered as the attempt to lay the rational foundations of an order of compatibility and cooperation among human wills.

In the course of the twentieth century, philosophical ethics or, as it is often called, ethical theory has become more and more a self-contained branch of study. While earlier systems of ethical thought like Plato's or Spinoza's tended to be developed in very close contact with the author's metaphysical, religious, or epistemological views, contributions to ethical theory in this century, especially in the English-speaking countries, have increasingly been worked out in substantial independence both from the other parts of philosophy and from the special sciences. Even in the case of logic, which has played a prominent role in the analysis of ethical concepts and reasoning, this generalization seems to hold, since the logic used is mainly of a very elementary kind which has not been affected by the major philosophical controversies in the field. It may thus appear that twentieth-century ethical theory or at least the most original developments therein do not lend themselves to a treatment in terms of intellectual contexts and especially not in terms of relationships of affiliation with general philosophical positions of the kind this chapter proposes to consider. And yet this appearance may well be misleading. For even when all pretensions to found a system of philosophy have been abandoned, broad philosophical movements may and do persist; and the conceptions of philosophical method and the styles of thought that characterize these movements can have a visible influence on the way such fields as ethics are developed and on the way their relationships to other areas of study are interpreted. Accordingly, I hope in this chapter to examine a number of broad movements within philosophy with a view to determining how they have influenced the way ethics has been understood and developed by the philosophers who have worked within them, and how these conceptions of philosophical method have set the relationship between ethics and fields of concern that lie outside philosophy altogether. Inevitably, my procedure here must be selective; and some contexts of philosophical thought will be passed over in favor of the three major movements of philosophical inquiry I have chosen to consider in their relationship to ethics: idealism, analytical philosophy, and phenomenology. It should not be supposed that these names stand for homogeneous philosophical positions that have been accepted by all the thinkers who have been associated with them. What they do represent are broad conceptions of philosophical method and of the objectives of the philosophical enterprise; and in one way or another, most of the significant work in the field of ethical theory in this century has been done under the auspices of one or another of them.

It is, of course, impossible to consider here the impact of these conceptions of philosophical method upon the treatment of the full range of problems that ethical theory has to deal with. I propose, therefore, to concentrate my attention upon the generic concept of ethics itself or upon what contemporary philosophers often call the "ethical point of view." This is usually understood to represent, in the first place, a logically distinctive form of judgment and an equally distinctive form of rationality by which a compatible order of human action is realized through common acceptance of universal norms which are understood to have a controlling authority for all rational persons. At the same time, there is associated with this notion of a moral point of view a certain kind of freedom, since an understanding of this form of judgment makes it possible for an individual human being to subject the conventions and institutional routines in which his life may otherwise be embedded to a form of appraisal and criticism that is expressive of his nature as a rational being. Both these elements—of rationality and freedom—are joined in the concept of autonomy, which has been a central one in twentieth-century ethics, although sometimes emphasis has fallen on the reference it makes to a law or universal principle and sometimes on the action of the self that its deployment implies. There have, of course, been ethical theories in which such autonomy is imputed to the moral community rather than to its individual members; and there has been at least one in which autonomy was virtually denied any significant application. Nevertheless, just these variations in the interpretation and use of the central concept of autonomy can serve as a thread of continuity in this review of the three principal philosophical movements to which I have referred; and it is in this way that I propose to use it.

I

Idealism, then, provides the point of departure for this study; and at the beginning of the century it was in fact the philosophy enjoying widest acceptance in Western Europe and America. Although it is often thought of as a paradoxical denial that matter or nature has any existence independently of consciousness, idealism is more accurately understood as an attempt to break down the hard and fast dichotomies of subject and object and to reinterpret the functions of mind as active and constructive rather than as a passive duplication of external realities. Idealism undertook to show that nature and mind are more intimately interrelated than the mechanistic natural science of the eighteenth century had appeared to allow; and in so doing it was responsive to a deep human need to interpret human life in a purposive way and to relate human purpose and action to a cosmic drama of some kind. Without in any way underestimating the subtlety of the logical and epistemological points by which idealists from Kant and Hegel onward have pressed their argument against the various forms of dualism, one may note that in many obvious ways idealism reveals its derivation from the Protestant religious ethos of which it is, in fact, a late and secularized version.

It is thus at first sight surprising that a philosophy that laid such heavy emphasis on human consciousness and purpose should not have made any very distinctive contribution to ethical theory as such. On reflection, however, it becomes clear that this failure was not accidental. Just because the idealists found development and purpose, and thus value, everywhere, they were unwilling to interpret ethical phenomena in specifically psychological or epistemological terms which might have a tendency to confine values to one domain of reality to the exclusion of others. If the history of the world centers on the history of consciousness as it moves from its fragmentary and finite condition in the natural world toward a final understanding of its own unitary and all-encompassing nature, as the idealists typically believed it did, then the whole subject matter of ethics must be inseparable from this movement of self-realization on the part of the individual and the cosmos. Just as, according to the idealist logicians, there could be no truth that was not a truth about the absolute, so in idealistic ethics, value and moral goodness are achieved just to the extent that the separateness and discreteness of our natural existence is overcome. The ethical ideal for the idealists must accordingly consist in some form of self-realization by which the implicit unity of mind with nature and of mind with mind becomes explicit and concrete in the form of some human achievement.

Applied to the traditional issues of ethical theory, these assumptions yield a position in which primary importance is assigned to the formation of relationships of cooperation and common purpose among human beings. Although these human associations typically serve to bring about the satisfaction of the physical and psychological needs of the individuals who compose them, their specifically ethical character is to be sought rather in the new and larger consciousness and selfhood they entail. It is not too much to say that the emergence and expansion of this larger collective self was self-justifying in the idealists' eyes, and they clearly regarded it as the real goal toward which all human effort, although for the most part unconsciously and by indirection, has been striving. The deepest ethical obligation of the individual is to this larger consciousness which he is to realize in himself and in his actions through his membership in some association with his fellows. Rules and standards governing human actions have their uses, but the idealists regularly resisted every effort to base them either on a calculus of human satisfactions or a conception of God's will that abstracts from the essential context of a human community of some kind. In the words of Josiah Royce, who was the most effective American exponent of idealism in the early years of this century, our deepest ethical motive is that of loyalty to the engagements to other human beings which we assume by virtue of our participation in the various forms of human association.[1] This loyalty in turn is not a function of self-interest or of the benefits we expect to receive from our participation. Rather, it rests on what Royce called a "loyalty to loyalty" and an essentially metaphysical conviction that self-realization requires the transcending of finite individuality in the interest of larger and social forms of selfhood.

The attempt to interpret the ethical life as the progressive identification of the self with larger human groups had certain implications that were at least indirectly normative. According to the idealistic interpretation, existing forms of human association, ranging from the family to the state, are bearers of the ethical idea, and the individual can realize himself ethically only by accepting the duties and the responsibilities entailed by active membership in these institutions. It was, of course, recognized that these institutions are imperfect and that their demands may conflict so that an appeal becomes necessary to a higher form of unity for which there may be as yet no actual institutional embodiment. But the idealists insisted that anything like rebellion by an individual against the requirements of his institutional roles had to be justified in the light of a more inclusive social ideal and not on the basis of a conception of individual rights that abstracted wholly from all social contexts, whether real or ideal. The point was that ethical progress could be made only through the very institutions it might eventually transcend or embrace within some larger unity; and the result was that one's duties as a member of a family or as a citizen came to be regarded as fraught with ethical meaning. The positive ethics of idealism was thus inevitably an ethic of "my station and its duties," as the English philosopher, F. H. Bradley, had proclaimed it to be in *Ethical Studies*, one of the few major idealistic treatments of ethics.[2] In faithfully discharging the duties of one's station in life, one could be assured of contributing to the ethical work of the world and Bradley, like Hegel before him, showed a special impatience

[1]Josiah Royce, *The Philosophy of Loyalty* (New York: Macmillan, 1908).
[2]F. H. Bradley, *Ethical Studies* (Oxford: Clarendon Press, 2nd ed., 1927), Chapter 5.

toward those who felt that they had been exempted from fulfilling these obligations by unique ethical revelations that bypassed the day-to-day life of families and states. One can say, therefore, that idealism proposed an orientation toward the institutional status quo which was broadly positive, although not uncritical, and which emphasized a form of personal self-realization that is the fruit of working within those institutions. If the latter are imperfect, they are still essential stages in the moral progress of mankind, and an individual must not allow his sense of their imperfection to take the form of a belief in his own moral superiority to them or a right to act independently of all institutional controls.

Insofar as idealism survives at all in contemporary intellectual life, it is mainly as a dangerous tendency of thought against which Marxists are continually warning one another. Clearly, the positive assessment of the institutional status quo which I have just described is a principal reason for such hostility to idealism; but there is another tenet of idealism that makes it even more objectionable in the eyes of social radicals and activists. This is the assurance that the conflicts between various groups and interests in society are the instruments of a deeper harmony which is on the way to realization; and that the negative aspects of social life —the suffering and deprivation under which so many labor—are not proof of the irrationality or the exploitative character of society, but necessary preconditions for the achievement of an eventual harmony of interests. There is implicit in such a belief a kind of cosmic optimism which many non-idealists regard as incompatible with a genuine recognition of the evil present in the world—an optimism which Bradley himself satirized when he remarked that "this is the best of all possible worlds and everything in it is a necessary evil." Such an attitude would scarcely have been possible for idealists had it not been for their conception of concrete human needs and desires as being merely the vehicles for a wider meaning or purpose which is realizing itself in human history and which in fact expresses the real intent of a fully self-conscious and consistent human will. To the critics of idealism, this amounts to an intellectualization and etherealization of human motives and concerns that can only be conducive to a sense of complacency about man's ethical situation and an incapacity to grasp the urgency of human needs. From the ethical standpoint, it is argued, idealism is not only quite unhelpful in determining what should be done, but it also incapacitates its devotees for such practical tasks through its general assurance that all is —fundamentally and metaphysically—well. Although it would be hard to deny that there is at least some truth in this indictment of idealism as an ideology of the status quo, one might reply that a different and more radical interpretation of idealism is not only conceivable but has actually found representatives in the history of modern ethics. But the fact remains that idealism has remarkably little to say that is directly relevant to the situation of the moral agent who must decide and act. Idealists exalt the will and the life of action, but in the final analysis they tend to leave the rational basis for the determination of the will a mystery, and to that extent their treatment of normative ethics remains contemplative and devoid of practical implications.

A defense of idealism as an interpretation of the ethical life can, however, be made along other lines. By refusing to contain ethical experience within the narrow limits of religious dogma or enlightened self-interest, the idealists gave a much broader meaning to the notion of ethics and made possible a multitude of new insights into the ethical significance of many aspects of human culture. This is especially true of the form of idealism developed on the Continent, which, in contrast to the American and British versions of idealism, laid great emphasis on historical consciousness and the history of human culture. There is always a strong tendency for ethics to be identified with a specific and perhaps quite eccentric and provincial code of behavior that enjoys official acceptance at a particular place at a particular time; and this conception can lead either to a blindness to the ethical substance of lives that are lived under other canons of conduct or to a wholesale rejection of ethics inspired by a feeling of disgust for the provincial and restricting character of the only form in which it has been known. In these circumstances the idealistic vision of the history of man as a great ethical drama can have a liberating influence on the imagination and the perception of those who have known only a much narrower historical perspective, and this conception of history as the ethical self-realization of man has in fact inspired a great deal of valuable work in the field of cultural history. There is, of course, a price to be paid for bringing the moral consciousness into closer contact with institutional and cultural history as idealism did, for when the ethically progressive character of the history it reenacts becomes problematic, as it has in our time, idealism may pass over into the kind of moral nihilism that is characteristic of some versions of existentialism. But the more serious charge that can be brought against idealism has to do with its evident incapacity to treat the biological and psychological determinants of human behavior as anything but material to be shaped and guided to a moral end by man's higher "spiritual nature." Here idealism seems to lose contact with its fundamental postulate to the effect that morality is not a special preserve but is as wide and inclusive as human life itself; and out of a concern to show the guiding role of ethical ideas in human affairs, idealism prematurely abandons the effort to show how these "ideas" are at work in the formation of human personality and in the organization and accomplishment of human work. Traveling the high a priori road, the idealists tend to treat all these spheres of material activity as expressions of the "idea" but without the kind of detailed examination of the relevant materials that would give conviction to these conclusions. What interests the idealist most, it seems, is the general assurance that the cultural and the ethical world are continuous and interlocking rather than the actual exhibition of an organic relationship between what he calls the higher and the lower spheres of human activity. This assurance is especially open to question when it is invoked as a defense against claims that there are in fact conflicts and discontinuities in the human world that are not resolvable within the medium of pure thought.

Perhaps the best known and, at least within his own country, most influential idealist of this century was the Italian philosopher, Benedetto Croce, whose intellectual career illustrates many of the strengths and weaknesses of idealism which I have been discussing.[3] By his unflagging energy as a publicist and polemicist, Croce made idealism and its ethico-political conception of the nature and history of man into a kind of working ideology for the Italian intellectual class, or rather for the bourgeois and secular wing of that class which was associated with the new Italian state and more or less alienated from the Catholic church. Later he also became a commanding intellectual figure throughout Europe, largely as a result of his refusal to take sides in the First World War. Croce came to philosophy—or at any rate to idealism—rather later in life, after many years of antiquarian research, mainly of a literary kind, in the history of Naples, where he lived all his life. This deep interest in local traditions was associated from an early age with an aristocratic disdain for the oversimplified and dogmatic ideas of the eighteenth-century enlightenment that attempted to define the nature and rights of man in virtually complete abstraction from both his history and his actual social circumstances. Perhaps Croce's deepest distaste, however, was reserved for all naturalistic and materialistic tendencies of thought and for the positivistic philosophy in which they culminated; and while he was briefly attracted to Marxism and socialism, and studied economics intensively, he soon reacted against this enthusiasm and asserted once again the primacy of mind and ideas in human history. When he finally came to a close study of Hegel's philosophy, in which this primacy was unambiguously asserted, Croce felt that he had finally found himself, and

[3]Among Croce's writings, ethical themes are especially prominent in *Philosophy of the Practical*, trans. D. Ainslie (New York: Biblo and Tannen, 1967) and *History as the Story of Liberty*, trans. S. Sprigge (London: Allen and Unwin, 1949). Also of interest is Croce's *Autobiography*, trans. R. G. Collingwood (Oxford: Clarendon Press, 1927). My view of Croce has been based to a considerable extent on Michele Abbate, *Benedetto Croce e la crisi della societa italiana* (Torino: G. Einaudi, 1967).

it was these idealistic positions that he was to defend for the rest of his life.

The paradox generated by the association of an ethical theory with a general idealistic philosophy is very clear in Croce's mature thought. This paradox consists in the fact that while idealism assigns to the ethical life a decisive and central role in human activity and in reality generally, this very interpretation of the ethical is subsequently invoked for the purpose of justifying a passive and detached contemplation of human events. This is a paradox because if human nature is not static but a process of self-realization, then there must be occasions on which the forward movement of spirit requires a sharp break with things as they are—such as occurred at the time of the Protestant Reformation, which Croce himself regarded as an essential step toward the achievement of the freedom and self-understanding of mind. Croce was very strongly convinced that neither philosophy nor ethics could anticipate this forward movement and that they could not give any kind of practical guidance or counsel to those non-philosophers who have to act and whose actions may change the world. What they can do, however, and what, in Croce's writings, ethical thought seems to be mainly concerned with, is to censure the error of those abstract and schematic thinkers who suppose that rules can be laid down either for predicting or for judging morally the actions of men. Thus the prime targets of his criticism are just those political theorists who seek to give history a determinate direction and thus confuse their own personal aspirations with the total movement of mind. Of the beneficent and supremely ethical character of that movement Croce apparently remained convinced, even during the darkest periods of war and the destruction of the secure European world he had known. He was most scrupulous in distinguishing his own political preferences, which he characterized as an expression of his social and regional background, from the philosophy of the spirit and of history for which he was a vigorous spokesman. But to many it seemed that Croce had thereby severed the bonds that connect theory—in this case ethical theory—with practice and that such an abdication of philosophy before the concrete ethical and political problems of the day in effect voided it of ethical content. Indeed, there are strong reasons for believing that a philosophy of the spirit which, like Croce's, is never willing to enter the arena of practical affairs and political conflict under its own banners and intervenes only to censure those who do, functions in practice as a conservative ideology.

I have already noted that idealism has been the object of a continuing polemic on the part of Marxist thinkers, but something more needs to be said about this polemic and about the Marxist treatment of ethics generally, which in fact reveals more traces of idealistic influence than most

Marxists are willing to acknowledge. Within the Marxist conception of philosophy there is no place for ethics as a distinct discipline; and the reason for this is not so very different from the considerations that explain the relatively undeveloped status of ethics as such within idealism. Marxists, after all, believe that the historical process is not only progressive and rational but also, within certain broad limits, predictable. They believe in the advent of socialism through the victory of the proletariat in the international class struggle, and until quite recently they have believed that the Soviet Union and the Communist party were the sole agencies of that eventual triumph. Marxists have accordingly not been willing to see in other non-communist societies any positive expressions of human achievement, and they have accepted as their supreme historico-ethical imperative the support of the one major communist society already in existence together with unambiguous opposition to bourgeois institutions as obstructive remnants of a type of society that is under the sentence of history. Under these circumstances, there has taken place within Marxist thought a very thoroughgoing "externalization of values," whereby the only ethical principle of universal validity is held to be that of furthering by any and all means the cause of the international communist movement.[4] The obligations of fidelity and justice which have often been represented as having universal human validity are treated by Marxist writers as elements in the non-universal class ethics of bourgeois society which have no claim to the respect of members of the proletariat and may therefore be violated when the class interest of the proletariat makes it necessary. In other words, the requirements of ethics and of effective political action in behalf of the communist cause are identical. Any attempt to formulate ethical questions in a manner that abstracts from the realities of political struggle is condemned as a form of "idealism," although the classical idealists like Hegel were equally distrustful of appeals to universal ethical principles. For the Marxist, ethics thus simply coincides with the policies that are historically progressive in the sense this notion assumes within the general Marxist theory of historical development. Sometimes Marxist writers give brief glimpses of the kind of society that will follow the establishment of communism; and it has seemed to many that they then reinstate many of the old "bourgeois" values that are currently repudiated. Nevertheless, these will then, in the Marxist view, be truly universal values, and in the meantime preoccupation with ethical issues as such can only have a distracting effect upon one's grasp of the requirements of the political struggle that is still going on.

---

[4] I owe this phrase to Professor Herbert Marcuse's *Soviet Marxism: A Critical Analysis* (New York: Columbia University Press, 1958), Chapter 10.

Marxism thus resembles idealism in the way it defines ethical progress in terms of the transcending of conflict among parochial human groups through the emergence of a universal class as well as in its unwillingness to recognize the validity of any moral criticism that abstracts from the requirements of the process that is to lead to that ultimate result. Of course, for the Marxist, revolutionary action is the means to the emergence of a classless society and this violates idealist predilections for gradual, almost imperceptible evolution. But in the one case as in the other the disallowing of moral criticism based on universal ethical principles tends to shield the institutional status quo, whether of the Communist party or of the Prussian state, against challenge. This Marxist subordination of ethical judgment to a hypothesized schedule of historical development and the instrumentalization of ethics it entails have been subjected to harsh criticism, not only from non-Marxists but from Marxists as well. The latter have pointed out that the original inspiration of Marxist thought was profoundly ethical and humanistic, and they have appealed especially to the early writings of Marx in support of this emphasis. But if there is considerable justification for the claim that Marx's condemnation of capitalist society rests on assumptions that are ultimately ethical in character, it is also true that he never formulated these assumptions and certainly did not acknowledge their ethical character. Indeed, from his earliest writings onward, his anti-moralistic attitude is very clearly in evidence, as one indeed would expect in a thinker raised in the Hegelian mode of thought. Attempts on the part of the individual to apply general ethical standards of whatever kind were condemned by Hegelians as unhistorical and abstract, and Marx was to share this adverse judgment on "moralizing" to the full. The justification of the communist movement, in his view, had to be "scientific" in character, and in practice this meant that it was made to rest on a distinctly Hegelian conception of the logic of history. This peculiar hybrid of unavowed ethical beliefs and historical predication is what Professor Karl Popper has called moral historicism or futurism; and he has argued that its general effect within Marxist thought has been to deny the ethical critic of communist society a *locus standi* and to substitute for ethical reflection and judgment a blanket justification of almost any policies on the ground of their historical necessity.[5]

But if the integrity of the ethical point of view has not been recognized within Marxism, there has been a steady current of Marxist and quasi-Marxist thought of mainly Western European provenience in which the claims of moral consciousness have been advanced, although usually

---

[5]Karl Popper, *The Open Society and Its Enemies* (London: Routledge, Kegan Paul, 1945), Chapter 22.

in Marxist terminology and without any effort to reinstate an undis-guisedly ethical mode of thought. An early effort of this kind was made by Gyorgy Lukacs, who introduced the concept of alienation as a funda-mental feature of the human condition under capitalism.[6] This concept of a condition in which the powers and achievements of human beings are no longer theirs but are controlled, like so many commodities, by the alien purposes of an economic and political system in which they have no effective voice, is implicitly an ethical concept, since it is tacitly assumed by those who use it that human beings have a right to determine freely how their energies are to be used and to benefit themselves from what they achieve by their work. Other writers like Leszek Kolakowski and Maurice Merleau-Ponty have analyzed the situation of the historical agent and have emphasized both the unavoidable uncertainty in which political choices are made and the personal and ultimately ethical char-acter of the responsibility such choices carry with them.[7] Thus far, how-ever, these attempts to create a larger place for the ethical situation of individual human beings within official Marxist doctrine have been largely unsuccessful; and their authors have either, like Lukacs, been forced to recant, or like Kolakowski, driven into exile. Only in Italy in the thought of Antonio Gramsci has there been any real acceptance on the part of Communist leaders of a more humanistic version of Marx-ism.[8] On the other hand, while official Marxism has remained largely impervious to these urgings, a very large number of intellectual dissi-dents from Marxism have been principally influenced by its failure to recognize its own ethical inspiration and to acknowledge criticism based on its ethical failures. The personal records of the many who fled Stalin's terror or left the Communist parties in the Western countries are replete with statements that reflect the influence of these considerations.

II

Idealism has inspired many critical reactions both within philosophy as a whole and within ethical theory. Almost all of these have denied the fundamental idealistic premise that truth and value are attributes of reality as a whole so that every finite apprehension of truth and value

---

[6]Gyorgy Lukacs, *History and Class Consciousness*, trans. R. Livingstone (Cam-bridge, Mass.: MIT Press, 1971).

[7]Leszek Kolakowski, *Toward a Marxist Humanism*, trans. J. Peel (New York: Grove Press, 1968); and Maurice Merleau-Ponty, *Humanism and Terror*, trans J. O'Neill (Boston: Beacon Press, 1969) and *Les aventures de la dialectique* (Paris: Gallimard, 1955).

[8]Antonio Gramsci, *Scritti Politici*, ed. P. Spriano (Rome: Editori riuniti, 1967).

must be partially erroneous. In the field of ethics some refugees from idealism like G. E. Moore developed a Platonic doctrine of indefinable value attributes which are the objects of distinctive cognitive apprehensions and are logically independent of whatever "natural" properties their bearers may possess.[9] This conception of the nature of value attributes was associated rather arbitrarily by Moore with the claim that, as a matter of fact, "good" is most often to be found in the experience of beauty and of friendship; but in some ways this part of his position was to prove more widely influential than any other. To be sure, Moore's acute dissection of the confusions of idealistic and utilitarian ethics as well as his positive account of "good" as a non-natural and indefinable quality inspired an immense amount of discussion, out of which much subsequent ethical theory developed, although along quite different lines. But it was the Platonic purity of his thought and his claim that the pre-eminent vehicles of "good" are beauty and friendship that account for his strong influence on a group of young English intellectuals which later became known as the Bloomsbury group and included such figures as Virginia Woolf and E. M. Forster. One of the most marked features of Bloomsbury ethos, which over the years was to be widely diffused through the intellectual class in Great Britain, was an aversion for public life and for what Forster called the world of "telegrams and anger." This revulsion from public life and the related attempt to build a private ethic of friendship was in notable contrast to the idealistic preoccupation with the public sphere, and it led to some bizarre exaggerations, such as Forster's remark that if he had to choose between betraying his country or his friend he hoped he would have the courage to do the former. Whatever the persuasiveness of this ethos of fastidious ethical privacy may have been, it never came to constitute in any sense a philosophy or a coherent system of thought and so it did not provide the kind of intellectual context for ethical theory with which this chapter is concerned.

By virtue of the philosophical methods he employed, if not the doctrines he defended, Moore *was* affiliated with a broad philosophical movement within which ethical theory has gone through a very significant and interesting evolution. It is not, however, easy to choose an appropriate name for this movement. Considered from the standpoint of the conception of philosophical method by which it is characterized, it might be called *linguistic philosophy*. The difficulty with this name is that some variant of the linguistic method in philosophy has been adopted by persons whose substantive positions in philosophy and more particularly in ethics differ as greatly as do those of Moore and Rudolph

---

[9]G. E. Moore, *Principia Ethica* (Cambridge, England: Cambridge University Press, 1903).

Carnap. It is, accordingly, not really clear whether linguistic philosophy, considered as a set of ground rules for the conduct of philosophical inquiry, has been in any sense the kind of semi-homogeneous context of thought that could influence the development of ethical theory in a univocal way. Certainly it has influenced the way issues in ethical theory have been presented and argued, and this influence has been uniformly in the direction of concentrating attention on the statements themselves in which ethical judgments are expressed as well as on their logical powers and their logical relationships to other types of statement. But even among those philosophers who agree on the centrality of language as the medium within which conceptual distinctions of all kinds are primarily articulated, there have been serious differences about the methods to be followed in carrying out these language-based analyses. Some philosophers like Moore and the later Wittgenstein have explored the logical intricacies of everyday non-technical language and have appeared to assume, at least as a working hypothesis, that the stratum of conceptualization they thus expose is both logically prior to subsequent scientific elaboration of the same materials and free from internal inconsistency.[10] Others like Carnap have felt free to dismiss common sense and its concepts in favor of new technical idioms of their own devising.[11] But again it is not possible to correlate this difference in any straightforward way with views in the field of ethical theory itself, since among the proponents of ordinary language as among the designers of ideal languages there have been significant differences on points of ethical theory. Accordingly, instead of trying to show that the "linguistic turn" in twentieth-century philosophy has significantly influenced the substantive content of ethical theory, it seems more profitable to turn our attention to some of the movements of thought which sponsored that "turn." Among these, none seems to have had a more important impact upon the development of ethical theory than logical positivism; and although it would be a mistake to identify analytical philosophy as a whole with its positivistic phase, there can be little doubt as to the pervasive influence on analytical ethics of the early positivistic theses about what is meaningful and what is not.

If idealism grows out of a philosophical reflection on human history and culture and thus shares the interest in purpose and value that is characteristic of the humanities, then positivism typically is inspired by the achievements and methods of the natural sciences. These are, in the

---

[10]An account of these views can be found in J. O. Urmson, *Philosophical Analysis: Its Development Between the Two World Wars* (Oxford: Clarendon Press, 1956).
[11]Rudolph Carnap, *The Logical Syntax of Language* (London: Routledge, Kegan Paul, 1934), Part 5.

words of Auguste Comte, who gave positivism its name, the positive sciences—i.e., the sciences that can predict and control nature and actually have substantial results to show while theology and metaphysics (the non-positive sciences par excellence) remain trapped in a labyrinth of words. To excerpt and generalize the methods of inquiry that have led to such success in the natural sciences and to use them as criteria for delimiting the sphere of what is to count as knowledge constituted the essential inspiration of modern positivism. In its inception, positivistic philosophy was thus not closely concerned with the ethical aspects of human experience. Consequently, its approach to ethical matters was programmatic and took the form of an attempt to apply very general theses about meaningfulness and the conditions of human knowledge to an area of experience quite remote from that which had first suggested these theses. The surprising fact is that in spite of this remoteness from questions of ethical theory and the negative character of its first efforts to deal with them, positivism has proved to be in many ways a stimulating environment for ethical theory, at least of a certain kind.

In speaking of positivism as a context of twentieth-century thought I have in mind primarily the form of that doctrine known as "logical positivism," which was formulated by the members of the Vienna Circle in the 1920s and later became very influential throughout the English-speaking world when the rise of Nazism compelled the members of that group to seek refuge abroad. This form of positivism is a lineal descendant of the empiricism of Hume, Mill, and Mach; it is distinguished from classical empiricism mainly by the status it accords to mathematics and logic as distinctive non-empirical forms of knowledge. Logical positivism, like all the earlier forms of positivism, was the sworn foe of metaphysics, which it sought to eliminate by demonstrating the meaningless character of all statements that are not verifiable by the observational methods of the natural sciences or by the logical operations that are appropriate to the propositions of mathematics and logic. There were thus to be two types of meaningful statements: the empirical statements that affirm some truth about the world and are verifiable by a form of observational procedure, and the formal propositions of logic and mathematics that say nothing at all about the way the world happens to be constituted and are true necessarily and in every possible world. Whatever is not classifiable under one of these rubrics must, according to the positivists, be literally nonsense even though it appears to be an intelligible statement, as so many of the statements of metaphysics and theology in fact do. Within the realm of meaningful discourse the positivists set themselves the goal of clarifying the logic of science; outside it, they made war on the pseudo-statements that paraded as knowledge while meeting none of its conditions. Especially after World War I, it seemed to many positivists that irrationalistic ideologies and all kinds of metaphysical humbug were gaining ground at the expense of reason and science; and in these circumstances the work of demystification they undertook had a clear affinity with the offensive launched by the eighteenth-century *philosophes* against dogma and superstition. As it turned out, however, the broader social implications of positivism were never to be developed in more than a fragmentary way; and it may well be that this failure is traceable in part to the treatment of ethics itself within logical positivism.

The application of the positivist criterion of meaningfulness to ethics in the writings of positivists like Rudolph Carnap was usually brief and devastatingly simple.[12] All ethical statements turned out to be meaningless, since they expressed no proposition that was empirically verifiable and certainly were not certifiable as true simply by reason of the meanings of the terms they used. Therefore, they expressed no proposition and could not sensibly be regarded as either true or false. There could accordingly be no such thing as ethical knowledge and no rational basis for the adjudication of the conflicting claims that have been made by different moral codes. Insofar as any positive evaluation of ethical statements was offered at all, the prevailing view was that they were expressions of feeling; and in its cruder forms this interpretation of such notions as good and bad was sometimes referred to as the "Boo-Hurrah" theory. It certainly did not lead in the direction of any further inquiry into the area of discourse it so thoroughly debunked, since what it conveyed more than anything else was the profound lack of interest in ethics on the part of philosophers who propounded it and whose principal concern with ethics was to make sure that it did not contaminate the logic of science in which they were really interested. But if this was the principal motive behind the positivists' attitude toward ethics, an even more negative evaluation of the whole topic of ethics seems to have been just below the surface. For what the positivists were saying was not simply that ethics has no epistemic credentials but that it has no credentials at all that could possibly make the expression of an ethical judgment more than an episode in the subjective biography of the person who made it. In a way, this is understandable, for where cognitively certifiable propositions enjoy such a monopoly of prestige and intersubjective authority, the making of an ethical judgment in anything but the most deprecating and self-descriptive way will naturally tend to seem rather like making a rude noise. What underlies the positivistic view of ethics, although it never quite gets said in so many words, is the feeling

---

[12]An excellent example of this treatment of ethics is A. J. Ayer, *Language, Truth and Logic* (London: Victor Gollancz, 1936), Chapter 6.

that while we cannot of course stop having ethical attitudes, it is best to be unobtrusive about them and to keep them in the background rather like a bastard child. Under these circumstances, it is scarcely surprising that twentieth-century positivism never developed a wider philosophy of society and that instead it concentrated almost exclusively on technical studies in the logic and language of science.

The above remarks should not be taken as denying that logical positivism, especially in its early phase, had a strong ethos of its own or that its conception of its wider mission had ethical implications. These were clearly evident in the thought of Moritz Schlick and Otto Neurath.[13] Schlick wrote a book on ethics in which he undertook to defend hedonism against the criticism philosophers have directed against it since Plato's day; and Neurath sketched out ambitious applications of positivistic ideas to social and political issues. Underlying the ethical and social thought of these two positivists and the less explicit assumptions of their more technically oriented colleagues was a belief that established the relevance of their philosophical views to wider human interests and suggested a nexus between logical analysis and social practice. This was the belief that metaphysical ideas, so far from being the delusions of only a small group of misguided speculative minds, had in fact penetrated the ways of thinking of ordinary people to a quite remarkable degree. More specifically, implicitly metaphysical ways of thinking were held to be especially characteristic of the rationales for the various forms of social, political, and religious orthodoxy. A vast enterprise of criticism that would bring positivistic criteria of meaningfulness and truth to bear upon these pernicious social myths was thus clearly called for, and it is such a critique that Neurath's work in particular projects. The suggestion appears to be that once the confused and sometimes positively delusional character of many of our belief systems has been effectively exposed, then our legitimate human needs and aspirations can be satisfied on the basis of rational procedures of cooperation and scientific planning. It seems fair to say that for the positivists there were no profound and enduring moral problems that could be expected to survive the demise of these metaphysical belief systems. Clear-eyed positivistic criticism could be expected to reduce them all to the status of manageable and perhaps even technical problems. This at any rate is the view that seems to be suggested in the most considerable work of social criticism that was to emerge from the general ambiance of the Vienna Circle —Karl Popper's *The Open Society and Its Enemies*, in which "piecemeal

---

[13]Moritz Schlick, *Problems of Ethics*, trans. D. Rynin (New York: Dover Publications, 1962); Otto Neurath, *Foundations of the Social Sciences*, Vol. 2, No. 1 of the *International Encyclopedia of the Unified Sciences* (Chicago, 1944).

social engineering" is proposed as an alternative to the allegedly totalitarian metaphysics of a Plato or a Hegel. A similar perspective is also characteristic of the social thought of Bertrand Russell, who was close enough to the positivists to be mentioned in this connection, and who was eventually to give up philosophical work in favor of political activism.[14]

The positivists' summary dismissal of ethical statements as nonsense or as expressions of feeling did not really satisfy even all those philosophers who shared their general philosophical position. It did not satisfy because it indiscriminately lumped ethical statements together with so many other kinds of statements that did not satisfy the canons of meaningfulness, and thus failed to bring out any of their characteristically ethical features. On the other hand, those who felt this dissatisfaction for the most part shared the neo-positivistic view that the proper object of philosophical inquiry in any field is the language and forms of statements in which the typical concepts of that field find expression. Accordingly, when Charles L. Stevenson undertook his pioneering study of the complex relationship between factual and attitudinal factors in ethics, he called it *Ethics and Language,* and thereby opened up a new field of logical or conceptual inquiry, parallel to the already established logic of science and mathematics.[15] It is out of this logical inquiry into the language of ethics that a number of interesting developments in ethical theory have come; and many of these new developments appear to break out of the framework of positivism within which Stevenson had begun his inquiries. Perhaps some of them really do; but I will argue that the widespread view that positivism has been completely left behind by the further development of analytical philosophy is only very partially correct.

The fundamental point in the emotivistic theory of ethics as worked out by Stevenson was the distinction between disagreement in belief and disagreement in attitude and the parallel distinction between the descriptive meaning of an ethical judgment and its emotive meaning. The descriptive meaning of a statement is the statement of fact it makes which may have to do with the feelings of the person who makes it ("I approve of *x*") or with some empirically verifiable fact about x ("*x* is sweet") or with some state of affairs that is relevantly connected with *x*. With respect to what is asserted in this descriptive component of a statement, there can, according to the emotivists, be disagreement in belief,

---

[14]Bertrand Russell, *Power: A New Social Analysis* (London: Allen and Unwin, 1938).
[15]Charles L. Stevenson, *Ethics and Language* (New Haven: Yale University Press, 1944).

and there are ways of resolving this kind of disagreement by means of controlled observation and experiment. But the attitudinal component in these statements cannot be analyzed as an assertion of fact and must instead be interpreted in imperatival terms. Thus Stevenson's first analysis of "*x* is good" is "I approve of *x*. Do so as well." The crucial assertion of the emotive theory is to the effect that between the statements of fact comprehended in the descriptive meaning of a statement and the imperative that expresses its attitudinal component there can be no logical relationship and therefore no sense in which such statements can be true even if their factual component is true. This was not to deny that ethical agreement could be reached by resolving disagreements in belief, but it was to assert that whatever linkages might hold between beliefs and attitudes, they must be psychological and casual in nature.

In some ways the substantive conclusions defended by the emotivists proved less important than the new kind of analytical interest they showed in ethics. Instead of dismissing ethics in a paragraph, they examined the logical structure of ethical discourse as a topic with a claim to interest in its own right. The very fact that this analysis could be carried out at substantial length and with very considerable internal complexity suggested a parallel between ethical theory and other, more respectable branches of philosophy, such as the philosophy of science. Ethical theory could apparently claim to be an analysis of the logical structure of ethical discourse in much the same way in which the philosophy of science is an analysis of the logical structure of science. This parallelism suggested that a principle of the division of labor that is illustrated by the distinction between the philosophy of science and science itself might also apply to ethical theory in its relationship to the ethical life. After all, the philosopher of science is not called upon to adjudicate the controversies between conflicting scientific theories, so why should the ethical theorist be expected to validate any specific moral principle or to be any wiser in the resolution of ethical problems in real life than the average man? In this way a virtually complete severance of ethical theory from ethical practice was apparently justified; but in fact a crucially important difference between the ethical and the scientific case remained. When it is said that the philosophy of science is not science, it is understood that the first-level scientific practice which the philosophy of science subjects to analysis is itself a set of procedures for reaching agreement about the natural phenomena that are under study. The philosopher of science does not normally intervene in controverted scientific issues because he has no better critical equipment than the working scientist for resolving them. But the abstention of the ethical theorist from intervention in first-level ethical controversies is quite a different matter. It is motivated not by the adequacy of the critical instruments that ethical discourse puts at the disposal of its primary users, but by their utter inadequacy as means of achieving rational agreement as distinct from persuasion. What ethical theory had accomplished, at least in its emotivist version, was precisely to demonstrate this inadequacy; and it could therefore scarcely play any role in ethical life except to urge the layman not to demand from the moral philosopher what the latter was constitutionally unable to provide.

If the short way with ethics of the logical positivists failed to satisfy even those who were sympathetic to its underlying philosophical motivation, a similar sense of dissatisfaction was inspired by the emotivist account of the logic of ethical discourse in which the rational and critical functions of ethical judgment received such scant recognition. As far as the autonomy of ethics was concerned, the only interpretation emotivism could give was an entirely negative one in which that autonomy was made to consist in the fact that ethical judgments are outside the controls that govern fact-stating discourse. Even such logical freedom in the formulation of his own principles of judgment as this might seem to confer upon the moral agent is heavily undercut by associating it, as Stevenson does, with a causal interpretation of moral judgment. The effect of such an interpretation is to incorporate moral judgment into a general psychological theory of the higher mental functions, most often along behavioristic lines, in which the element of decisional control over his judgments by the moral agent is scarcely recognized.

A number of efforts have been made to revise this analysis of ethical judgment in ways that would do greater justice to the critical and self-regulating powers of ethical discourse. An early effort in this direction was that of the pragmatists, most notably John Dewey.[16] Pragmatism had many points of affiliation and affinity with positivism; and it set its face against all metaphysical absolutes just as resolutely as did positivism. It retained, however, some of the philosophical apparatus of the idealism Dewey had learned from his first teachers of philosophy. More specifically, Dewey's concept of experience was that of an active, purposive interaction of the organism and its environment, both physical and social, that was very different from the collection of sense data with which most positivists had equated it. In this process of experience, knowledge and action were inseparably associated with one another—to know something was precisely to be able to control the environment in such a way as to open avenues for further action and the consummatory enjoyments to which successful action leads. In the course of meeting

---

[16]John Dewey, *Theory of Valuation*, Vol. 2, No. 4 of the *International Encyclopaedia of the Unified Sciences* (Chicago, 1939); and *Human Nature and Conduct* (New York: Random House, 1930).

and resolving the problematic situations in which their activities continually involve human beings, evaluative and factual judgments of all kinds are continually made in the closest possible logical interdependence with one another; and Dewey was convinced that there was no unbridgeable gap between the objectivity of scientific assertions and the alleged subjectivity of ethical beliefs. He was much more impressed by what they have in common and by the fact that both are subject to public control and validation in the light of the consequences that result from acting upon them. Experience for Dewey was thus a continuum within which "objective" status accrues to both ethical and scientific beliefs as a result of a constant process of collective experimentation. Interestingly enough, Dewey's own life seems to exemplify this conception of the unity of practical and theoretical reason, since he was involved in a great many activities, especially in the fields of education and politics, in a way that would be almost unthinkable in a contemporary analytical philosopher. As things turned out, however, Dewey's theory of the continuity between scientific and ethical judgments did not gain wide acceptance; even now when many of his theses are being put forward again in more precise logical terms, he is not given much credit for his priority in this field.

It is ironic that "pragmatism"—a term devised by philosophers like William James and Dewey, who were profoundly concerned with ethical questions—should have become a kind of code word for a policy of accommodation to existing realities and of not adhering rigidly to principles, whether ethical or otherwise. Pragmatism in this sense is often said to be a characteristic expression of American culture, and as such it may be enthusiastically received for the innovative and exploratory spirit it evinces, or viewed with alarm as a rationalization for adjustment to the status quo. Certainly there can have been no philosopher in our time who has argued more strongly than Dewey for an intimate linkage between theory and practice in ethics as in other domains of inquiry or who has been more receptive to the possible relevance the findings of the empirical sciences may have for both personal and social ethics. The charge that can perhaps fairly be brought against Dewey is that his conception of the reciprocal correction of moral principles by moral experience presupposes a framework of moral assumptions within which it works well enough but which is not in fact always accepted. Even under the more or less "normal" circumstances of American life in the early years of this century, Dewey's procedures for the testing of moral and social policies have been felt by many to favor, perhaps excessively, those virtues and values that are preeminently social and "democratic" at the expense of some of the less generally available and comprehensible forms of personal perfection. What is more serious, however, is the fact that moral experience in the twentieth century has not remained within the confines of such "normalcy" and that, in the age of genocide, appeals for flexibility and an experimental approach to moral issues fall remarkably flat. Within a sphere of moral experience that has been delimited by moral principles like that of justice—principles to which the virtues of experimentalism and flexibility are without much relevance—the latter retain all the value Dewey imputed to them. But it is surely a weakness in his ethical theory that he failed to acknowledge the conditional and secondary character of these virtues.

Although the views of pragmatists like Dewey were well known and had some influence on the development of analytical philosophy, it was Ludwig Wittgenstein's working out of a philosophy of language along what were in many respects pragmatic lines that decisively modified the development of analytical philosophy in a way that was to be of great significance for ethics.[17] In his earlier work Wittgenstein had participated in the effort of Russell and the Vienna Circle to design a language which would be proof against the inherent proclivity to metaphysics of ordinary language. (Indeed, in the Anglo-American tradition, only G. E. Moore with his "Defense of Common Sense" really held out against the disparagement of ordinary language and common sense which was almost universal among philosophers of the analytical orientation in the Thirties.) In important respects, however, even Wittgenstein's early work was marked by important departures from standard positivistic practice. In his *Tractatus*, which was often interpreted as expressing a point of view closely akin to that of the positivists, Wittgenstein had briefly characterized value and the ethical as lying "outside the world"—a world that was composed of atomic facts expressible in atomic propositions— and as therefore "inexpressible." There is much to suggest that this way of describing ethics was not intended by Wittgenstein as a final dismissal in the way that it was understood by the positivists, but there can be no doubt that he regarded ethics as beyond the range of language and expression and as suited at best only to some form of non-discursive and perhaps mystical experience. Later in his career, however, he moved away from his quasi-positivistic conception of what can be said and worked out a theory of linguistic and logical pluralism in which many "language games" other than the fact-stating scientific one are recognized as valid. He also came to lay heavy stress on the context of human activities—what he called "forms of life"—which gave these language

---

[17]An account of these developments can be found in G. J. Warnock, *English Philosophy Since 1900* (London: Oxford University Press, 1961). Their image on ethics is explained in Mary Warnock, *Ethics Since 1900* (London: Oxford University Press, 1961).

games their sense and to which the latter had to be related. Although Wittgenstein did not discuss ethics as a language game, the possibility of interpreting it as such was clearly suggested by his later work, and it was natural that the notion of working out the distinctive features of the "logic" of ethical talk should have occurred to the followers of Wittgenstein's thought in this later period.

The extraordinary response these developments in Wittgenstein's later philosophy of language met with was unquestionably motivated to a considerable extent by the challenge his logical pluralism posed to positivism with its very restrictive criteria of meaningfulness. Some commentators have in fact interpreted the neo-Wittgenstein movement as a kind of revanche of the humanist intellectual against the domination of contemporary culture by science and science-oriented philosophies that devaluate the pre-technological literary culture with which earlier philosophies had been so intimately bound up. There is certainly some truth in this interpretation, although the conclusion often drawn from it—that a philosophy motivated in this way is necessarily reactionary and pernicious—need not be drawn. Within ethics, the most marked effect of Wittgenstein's views was to emphasize greatly the social and public character of the rules that regulate and justify conduct, and to distinguish sharply, as positivism did not, between the regulation of conduct by reference to such rules and other kinds of controls over conduct, as against the kind of psychological theory that places all such controls—rational and non-rational alike—on a common footing. Efforts have also been made to invalidate the hard and fast positivist distinction between descriptive and prescriptive meaning and to show that ethical judgments are, contrary to positivistic assumptions, inferable from statements of fact. The imperatival interpretation of ethical statements has also come under criticism, and it has been argued that ethical statements need not imply any directive for conduct. The positivistic distinction between factual and evaluative judgments and the denial that the latter could be true or false was based on the belief that there was nothing in the world for such judgments to be about, i.e., no value qualities. This claim has been met by critics who have taken their stand, not in the way the positivists did on a matter of ontological fact, but rather on a scrupulously detailed examination of the ways ethical words are actually used. It has been persuasively argued that at the level of language the distinctions between fact and value that were so clear-cut and definite for the positivists are by no means as clear as the latter had supposed. In some sense, indeed, the old issue about the objectivity of value judgments that turned on the existence or non-existence of value properties has been abandoned, and in its place there has been introduced a conception of objectivity that rests entirely on the restrictions imposed by the internal logic of our ethical concepts on what may and what may not be validly affirmed in this area of discourse. These logical constraints do not allow very much in the way of revisionary or critical activity on the part of the individual members of the linguistic/moral communities in which ethical concepts and rules are operative; and the autonomy of ethics is recognized as the integrity and independence of the ethical form of discourse rather than as any radical power of moral self-determination on the part of the individual.

It is not really surprising that views such as these should have led some observers of the philosophical scene to conclude that a sort of reversion to idealism—this time couched in a linguistic idiom—is in progress. Complaints have also been voiced about what are held to be the markedly conservative tendencies of an approach to ethics in which socially recognized rules are apparently the only source of moral validity, and revisionary and critical activity on the part of the individual is very much at a discount. In fact, however, the current direction of analytical ethics does not bear out this prognosis of incipient idealism; and one may even wonder whether what was originally an antipositivistic counterrevolution has been altogether successful in avoiding the vices it censured in positivism. I have already noted a tendency on the part of the neo-Wittgensteinians to treat moral rules as though they were laid down in the internal logic of the ethical concepts enshrined in our language which we as individuals are powerless to alter. Now if taken literally, this conception of ethical objectivity can readily be accommodated by the positivist, to whom it remains open to reply that these facts about the articulation of ethical concepts in a given language or group of languages are purely contingent. He can simply interpret the philosophical inquiries that lay them bare as empirical investigations of a particular language system, and the logical relationships thus exhibited would thus prove to be simply a new set of (linguistic) facts over and above the previously familiar psychological and physical facts relating to morality. As such they would be no more capable than the latter of resolving questions about what is right when the question is not relativized to a given language system. The point here is that if one tries to insure the integrity of ethical discourse by abstracting its controlling norms from the way ethical terms are actually used in some existing linguistic community, the authority of such norms beyond the limits of that community and above all their critical function within it are not likely to emerge with any real clarity. One suspects that there has in fact been considerable ambiguity in the appeals that have been made to "ordinary language," and that the latter has been made to cover both the logical pattern of ethical talk in some existing linguistic community and the logical requirements of a fully developed system of moral cooperation which is probably nowhere realized.

In one respect, however, those who see a recrudescence of idealism in the philosophical work partly inspired by the later Wittgenstein may be at least partly right. There has been a clear revival of interest in the ideas of moral community and of practical reason, and while both of these notions carried a heavy freight of metaphysical implication in the philosophies of Kant and Hegel, it is becoming apparent that they can be profitably reinterpreted in contemporary philosophical terms. When analytical ethics establishes contact with these powerful ideas, its analyses of ethical terms are no longer ends in themselves and ethical theory no longer stops short at the limits of language. Instead it is free to consider the whole system of social conduct within which the language of ethics functions and to seek to define the most general conditions that must be met if any order of moral cooperation is to be realized. The goal of such an analysis would be to exhibit social relationships themselves and not just the language we use for talking about them as essentially mediated by certain conceptions of reciprocity and to show that the authority of rules is grounded in what might be called the logic of conduct. There is no question here of going back to an authentication by means of rational intuition of the cognitive claims of ethical judgments; but it does seem possible that by examining the forms of human relationship that subtend our judgments of obligation, the basis of moral rules in actual social practice may be made more perspicuous. It is also conceivable that such an ethical-cum-social form of analysis would at least facilitate the task of applied moral criticism since, even though no absolute standard for judging social practice is available, it would juxtapose ethical claims and ethical practice in a way that would make fraudulent and ideological approaches to questions of social policy at once more evident and more difficult.

III

The third general movement in philosophy during the twentieth century to which I have undertaken to relate the development of ethical theory is the phenomenological movement. Phenomenology is an outgrowth of the Cartesian and idealistic philosophies of the modern period of European thought; and its influence has until recently been confined very largely to the Continental countries, notably Germany and France. Phenomenological philosophy is no more a single homogeneous doctrine than analytical philosophy is. It is a general style of thought and inquiry, and like analytical philosophy, it has passed through several radically different phases of development of which existentialism in its several forms is the most recent. It is not surprising that the interpretation of ethics and ethical theory within the phenomenological movement should have mirrored these wider vicissitudes of the movement as a whole. The more significant phases of the movement, from the standpoint of ethics, are probably the later existentialistic ones, but these are not readily comprehensible unless they are seen in the context of the earlier stages in its development.

The phenomenology of Edmund Husserl was from the beginning an analysis of human consciousness, but it was also closely associated with investigations of questions in philosophical logic and the theory of meaning of a kind that one more naturally associates with the early days of analytical philosophy.[18] Like Frege and Russell, Husserl was a strong proponent of a rigorously scientific method in philosophy, and he was correspondingly hostile to the intrusions of views motivated by considerations of practical utility or moral edification. Under these circumstances, it was to be expected that ethics would play a relatively minor role in the development of his philosophical views; in fact his treatment of ethics in some of his recently published lectures typically took the form of an application to evaluative consciousness of the type of analysis he had worked out elsewhere. In its simplest terms, the phenomenological method was an attempt to disentangle human consciousness and its relationship to the world from all interpretations—scientific and otherwise—that rely on models derived from the way things behave *within* the world; and this pure consciousness was to be studied in its original form as the matrix within which the world appears. This world consists of different kinds of objects—material, abstract, animate, etc.—to which there correspond the different structures of consciousness through which they are intended. Each of these objects is intended under a certain description or sense which Husserl called the "noema" and which constitutes the essence of that particular kind of object. When this analysis of object consciousness is applied to ethical experience, the latter comes to be construed as the apprehension of a certain value quality that inheres in the object being intended, and it is important to realize that for Husserl there was nothing subjective about the quality so apprehended. In this as in so many other matters, Husserl was a Platonist, and he treated ethical values—those that call for some action on our part—as simply a subspecies of the genus of value properties. This form of value objectivism has a close similarity to the views that were developed by G. E. Moore and Bertrand Russell at about the same time and with many of the same philosophical motives. It was to receive its most extensive elaboration within the phenomenological movement at the hands of Max

---

[18]Husserl's major works are *Logical Investigations*, trans. J. N. Findlay (London: Routledge, Kegan Paul, 1970) and *Ideas: An Introduction to Pure Phenomenology*, trans. W. R. Boyce Gibson (London: Allen and Unwin, 1952).

Scheler, a philosopher who, unlike Husserl, was deeply and continuously involved in the moral and social questions of his time.[19] An intuitionistic theory of this kind remains the characteristic interpretation of value and ethics in the orthodox Husserlian wing of the phenomenological movement, although it is still a distinctly subordinate part of the whole phenomenological enterprise, as it was with Husserl. Only with the emergence of "existential" phenomenology in the work of Martin Heidegger and in the broader existentialist movement did themes of a generally ethical character come to occupy a more central position within phenomenology.[20]

There have been many interpretations of the existentialist movement which relate it primarily to a mood of disillusionment and despair produced by the social and political crises through which countries like France and Germany have passed in the course of this century, and more generally to the decay of religious belief and the peculiar spiritual homelessness that is said to be characteristic of the age of the masses. Although it is quite plausible to explain in this way the response that existentialism has found in wide sections of its literary audience, such an account is inadequate as a characterization of the intellectual motives of the leading philosophical figures in that movement. It would be more illuminating in this connection to bear in mind the points of affinity between existentialist philosophy, on the one hand, and pragmatism and even positivism on the other. The point to be made here is that existentialism is one way of coming to terms with some of the same intellectual developments to which pragmatists and positivists were also addressing themselves, and most notably with the wreck of speculative metaphysics and teleological interpretations of the world process. What more empirically-minded philosophers experienced as a welcome release from dogmatic restraints upon scientific progress had a very different and often tragic meaning for those who had more closely identified themselves with the speculative tradition of Western philosophy and who typically viewed the incoming age of "steam and democracy" without enthusiasm. Existentialism in the broadest sense of the term embraces thinkers in this second group who accept the "death of God" but reject the scientific world view as materialistic and deterministic, and substitute a metaphysic of the human person, often defined precisely in terms

---

[19]Most of Scheler's writings are not available in English, but ethical themes are discussed in two that have been translated: *Man's Place in Nature*, trans. Hans Meyerhoff (Boston: Beacon Press, 1961) and *The Nature of Sympathy*, trans. P. Heath (London: Routledge, Kegan Paul, 1954).

[20]Heidegger's major work is *Being and Time*, trans. J. MacQuarrie and E. Robinson (New York: Harper, 1962). *The Essence of Reasons*, trans. T. Malick (Evanston, Ill.: Northwestern University Press, 1969), also has a direct bearing on ethical issues.

of his unsatisfiable metaphysical aspirations, for the older and now untenable kind of cosmology. At the very end of the nineteenth century, Friedrich Nietzsche formulated a deeply original philosophy of man and of human culture out of philosophical motives of this kind, and became thereby the true progenitor of the philosophy which in its later elaboration was to be called existentialism.[21]

Nothing is more characteristic of Nietzsche's philosophy than his profound disdain for the demand for justification, proof, reasons, and all the rest of what he regarded as the bogus apparatus of moral rationality. In his view, only a sick will that is incapable of action in its own right needs such crutches; and Nietzsche very plainly declares the entire tradition of thought that seeks guidance for action in the counsels of a dispassionate and impersonal reason to be a pernicious fraud. The supreme monument to this sickness of the will is the idea of God as a supreme moral legislator and judge who, so to speak, does our work for us. But once he is dead, an immense effort of internalization is called for by which individual human beings are to appropriate to themselves the functions of moral legislation and emancipate the will once and for all from its degrading and paralyzing dependence upon the intellect. Since Nietzsche develops this theory of a new and truly autonomous human being in the language of myth as contrasted with the later jargon of ontology, its more precise implications on points of ethical theory are necessarily difficult to gather. Clearly, however, this is not to be a morality of general rules or of social cooperation and compromise; and Nietzsche very stoutly refuses to put up with any plebeian clap-trap about universalizability as a criterion for testing maxims of conduct. The blunt truth is that are *are* no "reasons" in the required sense for choosing a a way of life. It is chosen and, when necessary, imposed, and that is really all there is to say on the subject. One result of this wholesale rejection of logical controls is that Nietzsche cannot and presumably does not want to prevent the sphere of morality from expanding indefinitely to the point where it becomes coextensive with the sphere of human action as a whole. When this is allowed to happen, there is a strong tendency for our individual ideals and our personal conceptions of what we aspire to be to become the primary focus of the whole moral life. It is these ideals which we can be more or less plausibly said to choose; and when they are made central to the concept of morality, ethics as a whole takes on a strongly individualistic cast, since obligations to other human beings will come in, if they come in at all, only via the relation they bear

---

[21]Among Nietzsche's writings, see especially *The Genealogy of Morals*, trans. F. Golffing (Garden City, N.Y.: Doubleday, 1956) and *The Will to Power*, trans. W. Kaufmann and R. J. Hollingdale (New York: Random House, 1967).

to our own ideals. When the "moral" is construed so broadly, the private dramas of the self and the working out of the highly personal visions by which we order our lives count for everything, and interpersonal criteria of acceptability for very little or nothing. In fact the very gratuitousness of the choice by which I create values and give meaning to my world comes to be relished as a positive value.

To this morality of individual ideals and choice and to the ethos of heroic arbitrariness that is associated with it, Nietzsche made an immense contribution. In many ways, much of the later existentialism strikes one as a prolix scholastic elaboration of what he said, with a notable loss of precisely that flavor of personal authenticity on which such value has been set, and a serious falling off in literary quality. As I have already noted, it was in the thought of Martin Heidegger that Nietzsche's themes were to be reformulated so as to yield the characteristic theses of twentieth-century existentialism. The occasion for this reformulation was Heidegger's break with some of the central assumptions of Husserl's phenomenology, and especially with the latter's conception of the relationship of consciousness to its objects. Heidegger rejected Husserl's claim that the objects of consciousness are not truly and finally transcendent to consciousness but are constituted *as* transcendent within the immanence of conscious existence. He also drew a sharp ontological distinction between the being of things and conscious human being or *Dasein*; and his major work is an analysis of the structures of human being which at once opens on a world of things it apprehends as just existing and also transcends them in pursuit of goals of its own positing. From the standpoint of ethics, the most important feature of Heidegger's new phenomenology is its flat elimination of value qualities and its substitution of the notions of *Entwurf*, or project, for the older conceptions of ethical knowledge and ethical truth. In Heidegger's analysis of *Dasein*, or human existence, there can be no question of an authentication of our projects by reference to preexisting rules or truths of any kind. For human beings, who necessarily understand their situation in terms of some future outcome to which they have committed themselves and which they seek to bring about by their own efforts, there can be no framework of principles within which choice could assume its Aristotelean sense of a deliberation about means to predefined ends. In a radical sense, all questions about which possible course of action is to be chosen remain open and can be resolved for each person only by that person's actual decision, for which he then bears a unique responsibility.

Views of this kind would not seem to afford a basis for ethical distinctions among the various kinds of choices that human beings make; but it is apparent from Heidegger's account that an existential ethic would recognize at least one positive virtue. This would be a capability for living in full awareness and acceptance of one's ontological situation, and especially the radical freedom and responsibility it entails. Typically, human beings seek to suppress such self-knowledge and they do so by living in a public and collective medium which Heidegger calls "das Man," in which the personal character of existence and action is blurred by an illusory sense of there being determinate and preestablished norms that define the individual's situation and his action for him and thus relieve him of the necessity for radical choice. All forms of self-understanding that draw on the natural sciences as well as all forms of ethical rationalism must be included among the strategies of the inauthentic self; and it is extremely difficult to imagine any form of ethical consciousness involving shared or public standards of evaluation that would not fall under the same condemnation. Paradoxically, Heidegger denies that his treatment of this impersonal and public milieu has any evaluative implications, although its markedly negative character has seemed patent to most readers of *Being and Time*. Since no basis is laid for any form of shared ethical standards that would not be characterized by the obliquity Heidegger attributes to conventional moral consciousness, one is left to conclude that "resoluteness" is not only the principal but the sole existential virtue. But however admirable ontological courage may be, it is far from clear how Heidegger can avoid a nihilistic doctrine of action for action's sake, and these doubts are scarcely allayed by his association of his philosophy with the Nazi program at one stage in his career. Later he adopted a much more quietistic stance and the voluntarism of his earlier books is now apparently rather embarrassing to him. What remains constant, however, is the substitution of a certain posture vis-á-vis being for ethical consciousness in any of its more familiar forms in which the claims of other human beings upon us would be of primary importance. Heidegger's philosophy has significant implications for ethics mainly through its critique of the concept of value properties and its analysis of human freedom; but it does not make any contribution to our understanding of the moral relationships in which human beings stand to one another.

The second major thinker of this century who is usually described as an existentialist is Jean Paul Sartre whose thought, especially in his early work, *Being and Nothingness*, is manifestly derivative in good part from Heidegger's. Heidegger has, however, explicitly denied that there is any true affinity between his views and Sartre's "existentialism"[22] and he

---

[22]Jean-Paul Sartre, *Being and Nothingness: An Essay in Phenomenological Ontology*, trans. H. Barnes (New York: Philosophical Library, 1956). A briefer statement can be found in *Existentialism and Humanism*, trans. P. Mairet (London: Methuen, 1948).

strongly objects to what he regards as the humanistic character of Sartre's philosophy. There can in fact be little doubt that in one way or another ethical considerations do play a large and perhaps dominant role in Sartre's *Being and Nothingness*. In that work the notion of human freedom and moral autonomy is formulated in the most emphatic way possible, and the touchstone of the moral life is the degree of authenticity an individual achieves by an open acceptance and espousal of his own moral freedom. An even more distinctive feature of Sartre's work is his interest in the relationships among human consciousnesses which has found powerful expression in his literary work as well as in his philosophical writings. At the same time it must be admitted that the very possibility of ethics and of a non-antagonistic relationship between human beings based on a recognition of their freedom remains highly problematic in Sartre's magnum opus. His analyses there appear to show that the only possible relationships between two human beings are exploitative in nature and that all the schemes of mutuality that have been devised by philosophers like Kant really involve treating the other as a thing to be manipulated and controlled by one's own will. At the end of *Being and Nothingness* Sartre promised another book which was to deal with the ethical questions raised by the analyses of human subjectivity. There was at least a suggestion there that it might be possible on the basis of the new insights into human freedom afforded by Sartre's philosophy to transcend the alternatives of sadism and masochism in one's relationships with the other; and in other more popular statements on the humanistic character of his existentialism Sartre seemed to endorse this suggestion in the clearest terms. That work on ethics has never appeared, however, and in his later writings Sartre has attempted to work out an existentialist version of the Marxist philosophy of society and history, and has even adopted the Marxist way of talking about ethics as an essentially idealistic misconception of the nature of human society.

It is possible that Heidegger's apparent lack of interest in ethics and Sartre's failure to keep his promise to work out the ethical implications of his analysis of human subjectivity reflect a difficulty that confronts all forms of existentialism as they attempt to deal with ethical themes. Their distinction between fact and value runs parallel with an equally sharp distinction between the being of things and conscious human being, with the result that for the existentialists value must always be the expression of a first-personal act for which there can be no justification by reference to any state of affairs in the world or in man's "nature." But is there any way in which such free first-personal acts of choice can be compatibly related to one another in a way that is more than accidental? Since all the traditional philosophical efforts to provide a rational basis for ethical mutuality strike the existentialists as relapses into some illegitimate conception of ethical objectivity and thus as forms of in-authenticity, it seems very difficult for them to avoid ethical solipsism. That would be possible only if it could be shown that some form of joint self-determination or shared autonomy is possible on which an "authentic" and free society could be based, but such an account has not been forthcoming. The closest Sartre has come to it is in his theory of the reciprocity that characterizes certain revolutionary groups, but even this "group-in-fusion" turns out to be continually threatened with submersion in institutional routine and seems more a momentary experience of shared purpose with others than a stable basis for social life. The quietistic phase in Heidegger's thought which followed his unfortunate identification of the Nazi movement as the social expression of his conception of "resoluteness" seems to involve an abandonment of autonomy as a foundation for ethics in favor of a somewhat occult relationship to "being" which is conceived in distinctly numinous terms. In neither case has anything like an adequate theory of the social implications of the existentialist concept of moral freedom emerged.

Heidegger and Sartre are sometimes referred to as the atheistic wing of the existentialist movement, which draws its primary inspiration, as I have noted, from the thought of Friedrich Nietzsche. Another great nineteenth-century figure, Soren Kierkegaard, has exerted an equally significant influence upon that movement and especially upon those existentialists for whom some form of religious affirmation remains a live option.[23] Theirs is an existentialism that has not been touched by the phenomenology of Husserl and does not propose an analysis of the structures of consciousness. Instead, it takes the form of a critique of rationalism as represented by the great philosophical and theological syntheses of the past which undertake to interpret man's existence to him on the basis of a rational understanding of either the will of God or the logic of history. The prototype for such a critique of rationalism is Kierkegaard's long duel with the Hegelian system, but it becomes a polemic against the whole attempt of speculative philosophy to clarify man's nature and his ethical vocation for him on the basis of a general theory of reality. Of course, this kind of criticism of an ethics based on metaphysics must not be confused with the positivistic critique that was often directed against the same targets. Just as Kierkegaard, for all his hatred of the peculiar kind of complacency that he attributed to the

---

[23]Kierkegaard's most important works bearing on ethics are *Fear and Trembling*, trans. W. Lowrie (Princeton, N.J.: Princeton University Press, 1941), *Concluding Unscientific Postscript*, trans. D. Swenson (Princeton, N.J.: Princeton University Press, 1941), and *Either-Or*, trans. D. F. and L. M. Swenson (Princeton, N.J.: Princeton University Press, 1944).

Hegelian synthesis, continued to prize the human effort to relate oneself to the eternal, so the contemporary Kierkegaardian existentialist does the same. In the thought of Gabriel Marcel and Karl Jaspers, who are the most distinguished representatives of this type of existentialism, the world appears as broken or truncated because it is deprived of a relationship to the transcendent—to God—but the human tendency to see the world as truncated is not condemned as it would be by a positivist, on the grounds that there never was any sound basis for the beliefs that have now been disappointed.[24] Instead, the search for a quasi-religious meaning for life survives the wreck of metaphysics and rational theology, and in spite of its inevitable frustration, this highly personal and unsystematic search for meaning becomes the central element in a new characterization of human existence and human ethics. One might almost say that the linkage between ethics and metaphysics which could not be effected in a positive way is achieved by writers of this persuasion in a negative way, since the elusiveness of the transcendent objects of this quest intensify just those dilemmas and just those qualities of spirit in which man's ethical nature is now seen as being most perfectly displayed. Although it cannot be said that our understanding of ethical phenomena has been deepened by Kierkegaardian existentialism, its powerful portrayal of the multiple ironies and indirections of man's spiritual career unquestionably makes a contribution to moral psychology.

One of the most disappointing features of contemporary existentialism in all its forms has been its failure to develop beyond the original formulations of Heidegger, Sartre, and others. What has happened instead is that the vocabulary and philosophical style of existential phenomenology have become part of a kind of *lingua franca* of European intellectual life to which Marxism, psychoanalysis, and more recently a rather esoteric anthropology have also contributed. To the outside observer this syncretistic existentialism has a heavily rhetorical cast and seems designed to express the *Zeitgeist* rather than to serve as an instrument of continuing inquiry. More specifically, while the ostensible subject of much of this quasi-existentialist literature is man in those aspects of his being to which the natural sciences fail to do justice, it does not appear that the ethical dimension of human existence—surely of central importance in such an undertaking—has received much attention. In a

---

[24]Among Marcel's works, one should consult *Being and Having: An Existentialist Diary* (New York: Harper and Row, 1965) and *The Existential Background of Human Dignity* (Cambridge, Mass.: Harvard University Press, 1963). Jasper's *Man in the Modern Age*, trans. E. and C. Paul (London: Routledge, Kegan Paul, 1959) and *Reason and Existenz*, trans. William Earle (New York: Noonday Press, 1955) are of special interest in connection with ethical matters.

sense one may say that the tenor of this continuing existentialist literature is celebrative rather than analytical; and while the old idealistic confidence in the unique and prestigious status of man as a free and creative
being is gone, the idea of a distinct ontological status retains much of its
appeal even in circumstances that humble man's pride in himself instead
of exalting it. It has already been noted that in the view of some observers, neo-Wittgensteinian philosophy has become the "house philosophy"
of the humanist intellectual in the age of technology. It may be that
something similar has happened to existentialism, and that it has ceased
to be a living philosophical movement and has become instead a diffuse
idiom of thought in which the claims of individual human existence can
be somewhat vacuously honored and accorded the dignity which the languages of science deny them.

IV

In retrospect, the history of ethical theory in the twentieth century appears to fall into a pattern that is discernible within both of the major
philosophical movements, phenomenological and analytical, that have
been reviewed. Both appear on the scene as reactions against idealism,
and in the field of ethical theory this means as reactions against the
holistic and evolutionary character of idealistic ethics. The latter was an
ethics of community par excellence, and in it the human community with
the moral relationships that bind it together was held to be undergirded
and guaranteed by a kind of cosmic community of interrelated selves to
which all value and reality were attributed. The initial emphasis of both
successor movements was to dissolve the connection between value and
the absolute and to isolate distinct cognitive apprehensions of value that
would be self-authenticating. Within such an intuitionistic interpretation
of value, no special importance would attach to the social bond or to the
constitution of more comprehensive human communities, and apprehensions of value would be based on individual experience. Within both the
phenomenological and analytical movements this notion of a distinctive
value intuition was later superseded. In its place the imperatival and decisional character of ethical judgment came to be strongly emphasized
by the existentialists, while the positivists attempted a thoroughgoing
objectification of value phenomena by treating them as causally condi-
tioned emotive reactions. In neither of these interpretations of ethics did
its social aspect emerge at all clearly. More recently, however, there has
been a movement away from what many now regard as the excessive
individualism of such very different (and yet in this respect similar) positions of a Sartre and an R. M. Hare, and the idea of a moral commu-

nity is once again regaining some of the prominence it enjoyed under idealism, although now the metaphysical accompaniments of that older version have been discarded. In the case of analytical philosophy in its neo-Wittgenstein phase, this movement toward a new conception of the public and communal functions of ethical concepts has been especially marked, although somewhat compromised by its being presented as a descriptive logic of "moral talk." In the case of existentialism, the indications of movement in this direction are much less distinct; but they are not wholly lacking there either. The great influence of the late Maurice-Merleau Ponty has underscored the need for a conception of autonomy and creativity in ethics that is compatible with the patent fact of our dependence upon shared meanings and shared norms, ethical and otherwise.[25] Again, the general pressure of the structuralist movement in France appears to be in the direction of a recognition of shared systems of concepts and classifications in all areas of cultural life, and while there has as yet been no attempt to apply these ideas to ethical theory itself, one may speculate that this is the direction in which ethical thought may now move. It is interesting to note that this reestablishment of the idea of community in ethical theory coincides with a fresh wave of interest in the political and social implications of community which contrasts very sharply with the individualistic spirit of most political thought in the recent past.

This general pattern of development has not been confined to the philosophical discussion of ethical questions, but is also discernible with some modifications in the field of theology. There too, at the beginning of the century, the influence of idealistic philosophy was very strongly felt; and religion was interpreted in a way that emphasized its continuity with other aspects of human culture. Scholarly work in the field of theology tended to be conceived in historical terms, and although the tendency of much such work was to blur the lines that separate religion from art or politics or philosophy, this was not felt to be a disadvantage in the liberal Protestant intellectual milieu that inspired it. In these circumstances, it was to be expected that a strictly religious interpretation of the ethical life as obedience to the will of God would be enlarged so as to include the positive substance of social and cultural life within the sphere of the religious and the ethical. In a sense, idealistic theology of this kind really marked a dominance of philosophy over theology; and there was always a danger that, as happened in Hegel's case, religion would come to be thought of as a partial apprehension in poetic and mythical terms of the truths that philosophy, considered as a fully au-

---

[25]See especially his *Phenomenology of Perception*, trans. C. Smith (London: Routledge, Kegan Paul, 1962), Part 3, Chapter 3.

tonomous and self-conscious fulfillment of lower stages of thought, could alone clearly enunciate.

The most significant turning point in twentieth-century theology was reached with the massive reassertion of the otherness of God and of the discontinuity of religion with human culture in the thought of Karl Barth.[26] The notion of a general movement in human culture and history by which the human is gradually assimilated to the divine was abandoned in favor of a God-centered theology that cuts across human conceptions of goodness and rationality in much the way Kierkegaard's did. In such a theology the will of God as revealed historically to man becomes once again the touchstone for any ethics that claims to be authentically Christian; and the commands of that will are not incorporable into any schedule of the development of man's ethical consciousness. The effect of such a return to the revealed will of God is to devaluate radically the ethical claims of existing human institutions and codes that are assigned to the world of natural and unregenerate man. There is a certain similarity here to the existentialist treatment of all the ethical content of human institutions and practices as simply so many "facts" which leave all current ethical questions open. In both cases, it is being denied that the cultural-ethical world we have created contains any intimations of the direction of genuine forward movement, and in both cases the effect is to throw the individual back on the necessity to decide what he is to do without being able to depend for guidance upon either his natural or his historical milieu. In theological ethics, of course, the will of God occupies a unique place, both absolutely and in the eyes of his creatures, for which there is no counterpart in the existentialist analysis of ethics. Nevertheless, that does not alter the fact that a rejection of idealism has had the effect in both philosophical and theological ethics of giving a new importance to the notion of decision and to a conception of the moral agent as primarily a being who has to decide what he is to do and to be.

In this country the writings of Reinhold Niebuhr offer a good example of social criticism inspired by a generally neo-orthodox theological perspective. Its most notable feature is its sharply deflationary treatment of the moral pretensions of all the major systems of social practice.[27] An even more impressive achievement is the incomplete work on ethics that was left behind by Dietrich Bonhoeffer at the time of his execution by

---

[26]Karl Barth, *Dogmatics in Outline*, trans. G. T. Thomson (New York: Harper and Row, 1959) and *Community, State, and Church: Three Essays* (Garden City, N.Y.: Doubleday, 1955).

[27]A trenchant statement of Niebuhr's position can be found in *Moral Man and Immoral Society* (New York: C. Scribner & Sons, 1932).

the Nazis in 1945.[28] That work bears the clear mark of neo-orthodox influence on Bonhoeffer's thought; the central pillars upon which his conception of the ethical life rests are the freedom and responsibility of the human agent for the decisions by which his life is shaped and for which neither history nor nature offer any adequate warrant. By virtue of this intense awareness of the personal and decisional character of the ethical life, there is something of the Christian existentialist in Bonhoeffer. But there is also a real ambivalence with regard to the kind of autonomy that the modern moral consciousness claims for itself and an evident fear that such a doctrine expresses a new and exacerbated form of human pride and infatuation with self. For Bonhoeffer, these conflicts are resolved by the special relationship to the person of Christ by which all the actions and decisions of the Christian must be governed; he believes that in this relationship perfect submission is reconciled with perfect freedom. But the most interesting difference between this kind of Christian existentialism and, for example, that of Camus is that Bonhoeffer insists that the drama of the self must not become an end in itself or the principal animating interest of the ethical life. In some of Bonhoeffer's last writings in prison there are also suggestions of a movement beyond the teaching of his *Ethics* toward a radically new conception of Christian life in the world that would discard much of the apparatus of traditional "religion" and even, it appears, certain images of God. In the hands of some more recent theologians who have been influenced by Bonhoeffer's thought, this conception seems to reduce Christianity to an ethic of interpersonal relations, and that can hardly have been Bonhoeffer's intent. Perhaps it is not fanciful, however, to see in some of these late and fragmentary *pensées* an effort to express, without the distortions introduced by various metaphysical and theological beliefs, what the life of a Christian community in this world would be like. In such a community, bound together by the loving concern of each for each, the autonomy of the individual human being would of course find its place; but it would also have been so thoroughly absorbed in a life for others that it would no longer claim the center of the ethical stage as it does in most forms of existentialism.

---

[28]Dietrich Bonhoeffer, *Ethics*, trans. N. H. Smith (New York: Macmillan, 1955). Bonhoeffer's writings in prison were edited by Eberhard Bethge in *Letters and Papers from Prison*, trans. R. Fuller (New York: MacMillan, 1967), and Bethge's *Dietrich Bonhoeffer* (New York: Harper and Row, 1960) is the best account of Bonhoeffer's life.

TWO

ethics and the social sciences

*I*t is clear that within the compass of this book any general review of the treatment of ethical themes within the social sciences in the twentieth century would be quite impossible. All that can be attempted is to give some sense of the major developments within a few representative disciplines; and the ones I have chosen are political science, sociology, and psychology. The first of these—political science—is one of the "older" social sciences, the others being the law and economics. These disciplines have in common, besides their early emergence as disciplines, a close association—at least in their earlier days—with philosophy, and a direct bearing on social practice. In my discussion of political science I will have a good deal to say about twentieth-century jurisprudence and the theory of law, both of which in fact form an important part of the study of political institutions and ideas; and I will also glance briefly at some features of the treatment of ethical matters by economists which seem likely to have a wide influence on political science and on the other social sciences as well. Sociology was selected since it is the study of social man and his institutions in the broadest sense; and it was the founding fathers of sociology—Max Weber and Emile Durkheim—who propounded the fundamental theses as to the bearing of ethical values on social scientific inquiry that have shaped the practice of most twentieth-century social scientists. Finally, psychology, while not exclusively a *social* science, had to be included since it has developed the conceptions of human personality and of the human capacity for other-regarding behavior by which so much contemporary thought has been influenced.

I

What I have called the "older" social sciences—political science, economics, and jurisprudence—were widely regarded during the nineteenth century and earlier as forms of applied ethics, proceeding under very general ethical assumptions and responsible to eventual ethical appraisal. They are in fact still so regarded in some quarters, and it may even be that in certain ways there is more awareness now of the ethical dimension of these disciplines than there was at the beginning of the century. What has certainly changed, however, is the way in which their ethical aspect is understood. Although it is clear that this change has proceeded differently and from different motives in the case of each of these disciplines, a deeper similarity justifies treating them together. What happened in each case was that a certain traditional way of accommodating ethical elements within a branch of knowledge ran into heavy criticism and had to be either reformulated or abandoned. The commitment of these older social sciences to some acknowledgement of the relevance of ethical considerations to their work—a commitment that was not characteristic, in anything like the same degree, of sociology and psychology—undoubtedly reflects the expectation that these disciplines have a contribution to make to practice, especially in its public and social forms. That commitment has by no means been withdrawn in the course of this century, and in some ways it has in fact become stronger and more effective. Nevertheless, the efforts that have been made to redefine the relationship to ethics of these disciplines have left many questions unanswered. There prevails at the present time, in place of the old dogmatic assurance, a general receptivity to the idea of resuming a closer relationship with ethics, combined with anxiety about how this would be consistent with the integrity of disciplines that are understandably proud of the advances they have made—advances that many believe were made possible by the adoption of value neutrality as a prime principle of method.

In reviewing the state of the social sciences in the early years of this century, one is struck by what Professor Morton White has described as their predominantly formalistic cast.[1] The domains of social practice with which the several social sciences deal were conceived to be governed by certain quite abstract principles, from which particular conclusions for the purposes of social practice were to be derived. Although outright assertions of a supernatural basis for human institutions had become less common by the end of the nineteenth century, ethical principles as well as most broad conceptions of human nature and society still tended to be cast in an aprioristic and deductive form which suggested that they were to be applied, as it were, from above to the "facts" of human behavior. It was just this way of conceiving the relationship between the empirically discoverable motives of human behavior and these a priori principles that stimulated the dissent of the thinkers who mounted what White calls the "revolt against formalism"—men like John Dewey, O. W. Holmes, Jr. and Thorstein Veblen. As John Dewey put it, the error of formalism had been to deny that human nature, as we know it in the everyday business of life, was capable of generating the principles by which it is to be regulated. Furthermore, a refusal to recognize any reciprocal influence on one another of human interests and moral norms could, in Dewey's view, only result in the peculiar kind of split consciousness that encourages high moral pretensions and a low and static level of social performance. What the antiformalists in the social sciences were calling for was a turn away from abstract models—constitutional, legal, and economic—and a renewal of interest in the way men and institutions actually behave in these different fields. Underlying this view, there was a strong confidence that the natural motives and interests of men would not prove to be uncontrollably perverse or inconsistent and that, accordingly, to liberate them from such a priori frameworks would be an ethically and socially creative act.

If against this background one examines the evolution of political science during the first half of this century, one cannot help noting the rather static condition of that discipline and the persistence of the formalistic tendencies that were being challenged in other areas of social science. To be sure, major changes have been taking place in political science for some time now, but for the most part these seem to have been stimulated by developments in more active areas of social inquiry like economics and sociology. This is not to say, of course, that there has been any dearth of literary production in the field of political science, but it is interesting to note that in White's account of the revolt against formalism there is no major figure identified primarily with political science. In fact, for much of the period with which this study is

---

[1]Morton White, *Social Thought in America: The Revolt Against Formalism* (New York: Viking, 1949), Chapter 1.

concerned, political scientists remained primarily concerned with the formal structures of political life, such as constitutions, codes, and principles, long after other disciplines had become more sceptical of the value of such studies. This direction of interest reflected the close association of political science, on the one hand, with history and law, and on the other, with philosophy and especially ethics. The latter association led political scientists to look in the first instance at those features of political life that seem to represent the effort of a society to place itself under some general order of a rational and moral kind; and constitutional law not only seemed to be such an attempt but had also been the subject of a great deal of historical research, often of a high order, in the previous century. Political behavior, whether of groups or of individuals, was thus considered mainly from the standpoint of the legal and (implicitly) moral norms it might conform to or violate; it was rarely the subject of any systematic empirical study in its own right. Inevitably, the study of constitutional arrangements, when conducted under such auspices as these, had a partially apologetic purpose and tended to issue in a defense of either the democratic philosophy of government, as in the English-speaking world, or of some supra-individualistic conception of the state, as it often did on the Continent. Political science of this kind is really politico-ethical philosophy applied to the appraisal of actual political systems as these are reflected in their codes of law and in the formal structures of political activity. Typically, the conclusion of such inquiries was to show that the democratic form of government, for example, rested on certain beliefs of a philosophical kind—"the moral foundations of democracy"—and political conflicts, particularly at the global level, were interpreted as the expression of profound philosophical and moral differences. By virtue of this mode of analysis, such systems of thought were almost all, in a broad and untechnical sense of the term, "idealistic"; and their political complexion tended to be moderate, if not conservative, in respect to proposals for social change. Such radicalism as they expressed was usually moralistic in character and took the form of exhortations to live up to the principles of one's society in a fuller and more consistent manner.

The foregoing is a much too brief and therefore somewhat unfair summary characterization of a large but diverse group of political theorists. In the absence of any really original political philosophy, its main achievements are probably to be found in the work done in the history of political thought, to which a role of commanding importance in political life and history was often assigned. Perhaps more interesting are the connections between this theoretical approach to political matters and a certain style of statesmanship of which there have been many exemplars, especially in the English-speaking world, in the course of this century and the last. Woodrow Wilson, who came to politics from the teaching of political science, was perhaps the supreme example of this style, of which the hallmark is a rigid insistence on the priority of moral considerations in the conduct of politics, both domestic and foreign. It is a style which has been called "moralism" by George Kennan, who observed at first hand what he regarded as its unfortunate consequences in the diplomatic sphere; and this same strain of high-minded idealism has found perceptive critics in other writers like Hans Morgenthau and Reinhold Niebuhr.[2] The critique of moralism in politics which these writers have mounted rests on the charge that an obsession with moral goals induces a certain blindness to what is in fact taking place in the world of nations and parties, and especially to the consequences of the policies that are pursued on these a priori moral grounds. In Kennan's view, there has been a disastrous tendency on the part of American statesmen to subscribe to principles in the abstract and to assume that the rightness of the principle guarantees the goodness of the consequences its adoption brings about, although in fact the play of national interests may distort the initial intent of the policy out of all recognition. The alternative to moralism that such critics propose is not always clear; but at the very least it calls for a realistic recognition of what the operative interests and motives in the political arena are and what outcomes they will tend to produce, as well as a more modest and realistic temper of mind in those who seek to impose a moral order on a recalcitrant world. For some, the balance of power has acquired a new prestige as defining a sane and achievable goal for statesmanship, and this has brought charges of cynicism and indifference to the great moral tasks to which this country is called. But a juster reading of the intentions of writers like Kennan would suggest that they are not really calling for an abandonment of all moral controls over political action, but for what in another context has been called a "morality of morality"—that is, a willingness to look at one's own morally inspired undertakings and at their impact on others and to moderate the intensity of one's idealism in the light of an honest appraisal of its likely consequences.

The most significant breaks with the conception of law and the political order that I have been outlining were effected not by political scientists but by students of the law, and more specifically by two movements of thought in the early part of the century which sharply challenged conventional views of the moral presuppositions of the law. The

---

[2]George F. Kennan, *American Diplomacy 1900–1950* (Chicago: University of Chicago Press, 1951); Hans Morgenthau, *Politics in the Twentieth Century* (Chicago: University of Chicago Press, 1962); and H. R. Davis and R. C. Good, eds., *Reinhold Niebuhr on Politics* (New York: Scribner, 1960).

86 / hair hair need to be
in context — —
ERIC Heller

G Thesis.
(i) Traditionally — Authority —
A " common good
Personal virtue
" Goal g human history
→ 20 Th Cent
K " Serious doubts" After 19
The 20 Cent
" Doubts' become
common grounds g intell
life
Lit → acterew Than histories.
POV

first of these, legal realism, was of largely American origin, and it was in fact the outcome of an application of antiformalistic views to the analysis of the law. There, if anywhere, the vices of formalism were glaringly obvious in the form of the doctrine that the law somehow exists as a fully determinate logical structure in advance of judicial interpretation, and that legal decisions owe their validity to their deduction from the law in this supra-temporal and supra-historical sense. It was this conception of the law that legal realism held up to a critical scrutiny that typically took the form of questions about the role of the judge and about the decisions through which the law becomes concrete and specific for those who appear before him. On the other hand, the legal realist points out that as a matter of fact a judge's decision is not so constrained by the statutory law it applies as to be deducible from it. Instead it is made in a way that can be understood only if one bears in mind, in addition to the constraints of statutory law and previous judicial decisions, the economic and political circumstances of the time and the characteristic attitudes and cast of mind of the judge. On the other hand, the realist does not simply regard these facts about judicial behavior as deplorable realities with which a practicing lawyer must willy-nilly reckon. He tends rather to drop altogether the notion of judicial decision as being bound by antecedent rules, and argues that in the nature of the case a judge, however great his respect for antecedent law, typically finds himself in the position of resolving issues for which the law gives no adequate guidance. He is thus himself a legislator; and therefore the best-known dictum of the legal realists—that the law is what the courts declare it to be—must be treated not as an expression of cynicism but as a serious analysis of the concept of law. In keeping with the antiformalistic spirit, the law is no longer to be thought of as an isolated and autonomous system of norms, but as a continuing process of decision in which the paramount attitudes and concerns of society find expression.

In a real sense the effect of this analysis is to undermine the distinction between the legal and moral, since the two are held to be inextricably associated with one another in the judicial decision. This conclusion was congenial to many who hoped that as a result the law could be used more freely to realize socially beneficial ends. But if the judge is of necessity both a legislator and a moralist, there is a real danger that his decisions will be regarded as expressions of an arbitrary personal fiat unless a wider moral basis for them can be persuasively demonstrated. In the work of some of the great American jurists like Louis D. Brandeis and Learned Hand, such a broadly conceived moral standpoint was adumbrated but it has not been elaborated in any systematic way. It is not surprising, therefore, that the insights of legal realism have borne fruit chiefly in somewhat cynical, psychologizing interpretations of judicial practice in the manner of Thurman Arnold and Jerome Frank, in which the moral attitudes reflected in judicial decisions are represented as simply the personal preferences of the judge.[3] In the popular mind, the image of the law so created typically provokes unfavorable reactions on the ground that such preferences are inevitably political, and there have been many appeals for a return to stricter rules of constitutional interpretation which do not allow such leeway for the personal predilections of the judge. Beyond this rather sterile contrast of judicial subjectivity, on the one hand, and a rigidly conceived judicial neutrality on the other, the controversies set off by the legal realists do not appear to have moved. The courts and the law generally are now widely understood to be responsive to political and social pressures; but if there is a moral basis for judicial interpretation—a morality which is neither individual whim nor a priori truth—it has not achieved a coherent statement in the writings of the legal realists.

The general philosophical background for legal positivism—the second of the two movements referred to earlier—has already been provided by the review of positivism in the last chapter. Legal positivism developed principally in Europe, and although it is often supposed to have a clear affinity with American realism, the differences between the two, and especially the much greater philosophical rigor of the positivists, are very evident. In the pure theory of law of the Austrian jurist, Hans Kelsen— by all odds the most vigorous proponent of legal positivism—many of the rather ambiguous formulations of the relationship of law to morality on the part of the legal realists were replaced by uncompromising positivistic doctrine.[4] Kelsen's writings are in effect one sustained polemic against the theory of natural law in all its forms; he emphatically rejects the central claim that this theory makes—the claim that moral and value judgments are susceptible of truth and falsity and thus express a form of objective knowledge. But if morality cannot be infused into the law at the top through certain supreme norms that are at once legal and moral, neither can it come in at the bottom via judicial decisions, since in Kelsen's view any moral elements in those decisions are strictly "irrational" and are no more susceptible of cognitive authentication than are abstract maxims like "To each his own." Since there are no criteria that are both rational and moral, the definition of law must abstract altogether from substantive moral distinctions and must be stated in purely formal terms. A norm of conduct qualifies as a legal norm only if it is made or adopted

---

[3]Thurman Arnold, *The Symbols of Government* (New Haven: Yale University Press, 1935) and *The Folklore of Capitalism* (New Haven: Yale University Press, 1937); and Jerome Frank, *Law and the Modern Mind* (New York: Brentano, 1930).
[4]Kelsen's major work is *General Theory of Law and State*, trans. A. Wedberg (Cambridge, Mass.: Harvard University Press, 1945).

in a certain way stipulated by another norm, which Kelsen calls the basic norm. This basic norm may be laid down in a written constitution as a rule governing the way other rules are to be made, or it may be implicit in the law-making procedures of some society from which it is extracted in the form of a postulate by the legal philosopher. In any case both legislatures and judges act under the auspices of this basic norm, and the latter produce particular norms through the decisions they give in specific cases by applying the norms created by legislation. Kelsen does not claim that these decisions are always logically derivable from statute law, although he has none of the antipathy for systems of logically interrelated norms that was so characteristic of the legal realists. But he does regard the legal order that is created by the proliferation of norms in accordance with the basic norm as complete and autonomous, and he interprets the concept of the state as that of a population and a territory in which such a legal system is operative and in which a monopoly of coercive sanctions is claimed for that system.

It is not easy to assess the implications in practice of this conception of the relationship between law and morality. As I have noted, the positivists do not see the judicial decision as the point at which moral considerations shape the law, whether legitimately or illegitimately; generally the legal system is endowed by them with a degree of impersonal reality for both judge and citizen which is lacking in the account given by the realists. Moral beliefs can influence the law, according to the positivists, only at those occasions stipulated in the law itself, on which the citizen, whether as voter or legislator, is called upon to express a preference. As to the substantive content the law takes on through such collective choices, as well as the frequency with which such choices can be made and the scope they are allowed, the pure theory of law declares itself to be entirely neutral. No doubt it *is* neutral as between conflicting political philosophies, but in its own way it nevertheless subtly prejudges the relationship between law and morals. For on its terms, the "inputs" individuals make through voting or otherwise to this formally regulated system are necessarily lacking in any distinct moral authority, and it is only through enactment into law that the attitudes they represent acquire a genuine title to public compliance. It follows that the position of the critic of the law and more particularly of the critic who seeks to hold the law to some moral standard will, as interpreted by the pure theory of law, be a very weak one. The only publicly recognized authority in this domain of human action will be that of the positive law; and by comparison the ethically motivated objections that are brought against such positive law will be able to claim only the warrant of individual preference. The contest between the legal "ought" and the moral "ought" will under these conditions be a conspicuously unequal one.

The conceptions of the law discussed so far were developed, for the most part, before World War II. The events of the Thirties and Forties and especially the massive and appalling denial of elementary human rights by the political regimes of Hitler and Stalin provoked a strong reaction in many minds against philosophies of law which certainly did not sanction these enormities but did not appear to provide any basis for condemning them on moral grounds either. Thus, the failure of the German legal profession to offer any effective resistance to Nazism has been attributed to the separation of law and morals in positivistic jurisprudence, although in fairness it should be pointed out that other and perhaps more deeply rooted German attitudes toward the state and social authority generally may have disarmed ethical criticism of Nazi "law" even more effectively than positivism. In any case, in the post-war period, dissatisfaction with legal positivism led to a revival of interest in the theory of natural law in which the priority of ethical considerations is unambiguously asserted. In Germany itself, the well-known jurist, Gustav Radbruch, who had formerly defended a relativistic and at least semi-positivistic conception of the law, declared his conviction that some form of natural law was an indispensable presupposition of legal thought; and there is some evidence that German courts in the post-war period have based decisions on what is asserted to be a higher, i.e., an ethical law.[5] The International Tribunal for War Crimes at Nuremberg very clearly committed itself to a doctrine of the responsibility of all human beings to withhold obedience to their superiors when the latter commit crimes against humanity; but no attempt was made to characterize the conception of ethics on which this requirement rested. Elsewhere there has been a renewed interest in Thomistic versions of the natural law doctrine, but this has not led to any major or original restatement of that view. In the field of analytical jurisprudence there have been more modest efforts to argue for an affinity between law and morals that goes beyond what strict Kelsenian positivism would allow. Thus, Professor Lon Fuller has sought to demonstrate that certain very general procedural principles of the law such as publicity and consistency compose a kind of internal morality of the law which falls short of being a set of ethical absolutes in the natural law sense, but nevertheless suffices to disqualify the enactments of a criminal government as law and thus provides a basis for a refusal to obey.[6] In another vein, Professor H. L. A. Hart, who otherwise favors the kind of working distinction between law

---

[5]For a discussion of this issue with bibliographical references, see Lon L. Fuller, "Positivism and Fidelity to Law," *Harvard Law Review*, Vol. 71 (1958), 630–72. The companion article by H. L. A. Hart, "Positivism and the Separation of Law and Morals," *ibid.*, 593–629, is also of interest.

[6]Lon L. Fuller, *The Morality of Law* (New Haven: Yale University Press, 1964).

and morality for which Bentham and Austin stood, has spoken of a partial overlap of systems of moral and legal rules, and has emphatically asserted the priority of the former over the latter, at least in circumstances like those that prevailed during the Nazi period.[7] Most recently, events in the United States, and most notably the war in Vietnam and the racial crisis, have given great urgency to the issue of civil disobedience and have stimulated public discussion of the moral basis for disobedience to constituted civil authorities. On the whole, however, it seems that this renewal of interest in the ethical foundations of law and public policy has not found expression in any substantial philosophical reinterpretation of the relationship between law and morality. A sense of the urgency of the issues involved certainly exists, and the intellectual climate is much more hospitable to efforts to associate moral and legal considerations with one another than it has been in the recent past. But in the absence of a comprehensive and persuasive reformulation of the doctrine of the ethical functions of the law, the de facto autonomy and self-sufficiency of the legal sphere tends to reassert itself, and efforts to enforce the claims of the ethical consciousness have the character of personal initiatives rather than that of well-founded doctrine.

The impact upon political science as a whole of these developments within legal theory was undoubtedly significant, but probably not as great as that of a rather differently motivated critique of the older tradition of political science in which a number of European thinkers reformulated arguments similar to those of the legal realists in a more radical way. Although there is no single name for this set of ideas, it was stimulated by a fundamental revision in the view taken of the role of ideas in social life generally—a revision which was first carried out by renegade philosophers like Marx and Nietzsche in the last century and became widely influential in the scientific study of society in this one. The central concept in which these new tendencies of thought came to a head was that of "ideology"; and I will have a good deal more to say about that concept later in this chapter. By way of brief characterization, one may say that ideas and belief systems come to be thought of as "ideologies" partly as a result of sceptical doubts about the possibility of specifying truth conditions for philosophical and moral beliefs and partly under the influence of a conception of the economic function of mind that was borrowed from evolutionary biology. Ideas are interpreted by reference to the situation of those who use them and the pragmatic function they serve within the vital economy of some group or class. Very often, too, the genesis of these ideas is explained, as it was by Marx and Nietzsche, as a projection or coded symbol of some real states of affairs

---

[7]H. L. A. Hart, *The Concept of Law* (Oxford: Clarendon Press, 1964).

which may be variously conceived in psychological or sociological terms and which the person entertaining these ideas may not recognize or at least not recognize as having any relationship to his own beliefs. There is no form of belief that is necessarily immune to this kind of analysis, but it is clear that scientific beliefs will be less susceptible to treatment in such terms than are religious, political, and moral beliefs. Moreover, the most significant implication of the use of the concept of ideology is that such beliefs are not profitably appraised on their own terms or on the assumption that they have a determinable truth value. Many political scientists have accordingly tended to discount heavily as "ideology" the very elements of predominantly moral philosophy to which their predecessors had attributed such importance. While it might be conceded that ideological beliefs were more than the "superstructure" erected on the basis of economic relationships and might have some independent impact on the way people behave, the idea that an ideology might be in some sense objectively valid and suited for use as an instrument of criticism of social practice was virtually excluded by the internal logic of the concept of ideology itself.

The literature of political science, which in one way or another reflects these views, is vast and highly diverse. In the early years of the century, the conviction that ideas are somehow comprehensively in the service of "life" or the "will" led to the elaboration of various theories of the political role of myth among which Georges Sorel's analysis of the "myth of the general strike" is probably the best known.[8] In some instances, a personal enthusiasm for one or another of these political myths would sweep a political thinker along in some great mass movement like Fascism in which the cult of irrationality was especially strong. More prudent and dispassionate minds pursued their interest in ideology into other fields like sociology and psychology, where it was thought the ultimate determinants of belief might be found; and here Karl Mannheim produced the closest thing to a general theory of ideology in this century.[9] But more often than not the premise on which work of this kind rests has to do with the non-rational character of man as a political actor or participant, and it simply assumes that political ideas and discourse as such are inevitably the creatures of non-rational interests and passions and lack any criterion of truth or validity on which moral criticism of the political order might rely. For the most part, political scien-

---

[8]Georges Sorel, *Reflections on Violence*, trans. T. E. Hulme (New York: P. Smith, 1946). An excellent article on "Georges Sorel" by Isaiah Berlin appeared in the *Times Literary Supplement*, 31 December 1971 (No. 3, 644).
[9]Karl Mannheim, *Ideology and Utopia* (London: K. Paul, Trench, Trubner and Co., 1936).

tists have made this assumption on general philosophical grounds such as those that purport to show the underivability of "ought" statements from "is" statements, and there have been few attempts to justify these sceptical conclusions through a careful examination of the logic of the principal systems of political philosophy.

At the same time political scientists were revising their views about the importance of philosophical and ethical thought within their inquiries, there was also a sharp uptake in the interest they showed in political behavior. Political systems were evidently not the same thing as constitutional systems; the deviations of political behavior from the norms of constitutional law may be of independent interest and deserve study in their own right. Once released from the ethical assumptions characteristic of the older political science, students of political behavior reverted to a yet older tradition—that of Machiavelli and Spinoza—and assumed that the animating motive of political behavior is the desire for power. Perhaps the general tendency of this new approach is conveyed best by the title of a book by Harold Lasswell, one of the leading figures in this movement: *Politics: Who Gets What, When, How.*[10] In other words, the subject matter of political science is not to be simply the operation of the political system more or less in accordance with the codes of constitutional law, but the whole struggle for positions of relative advantage in relation to one another in which all human beings are engaged and on which all the benefits they enjoy depend. Especially in its European versions, as for example the thought of the Italian political scientist Gaetano Mosca, this essentially non-normative interest in the way *homo politicus* behaves was associated with the view that the outcome of this struggle must always be the centralization of power in an oligarchy of some kind —a view that quite unfairly led to Mosca's being attacked as an apologist for Fascism.[11] In general, however, many of the "New Machiavellians," as James Burnham called them, seem to have believed that the realism with which they studied political behavior was not only consistent with their own democratic political preferences but might serve the cause of democracy better than the moralism of the older tradition had done. Thinkers of this persuasion may recognize that political science is a policy science, but its role appears to be understood in purely instrumental terms, and the goals to which the insights gathered from the value-free inquiries of political science are eventually harnessed are

---

[10]Harold Lasswell, *Politics: Who Gets What, When, How* (New York: P. Smith, 1950). See also H. Lasswell and A. Kaplan, *Power and Society* (New Haven: Yale University Press, 1950).
[11]Gaetano Mosca, *The Ruling Class*, trans. H. Kahn (New York: McGraw Hill, 1939).

to be contributed by extra-disciplinary "value judgments." These are often explicitly declared by writers in this field and may very well be drawn from the democratic ethic; but an examination of such judgments is treated as falling outside the scope of positive political theory and as having little influence on the way political behavior is conceptualized for the purposes of such theory.

It has often been pointed out that the twentieth century has failed to produce any original political philosophy; and this fact has been made a matter of reproach to the professional students of political affairs. In the light of the developments that have just been reviewed, this failure can scarcely occasion surprise, since their effect has been to make all views of the desirable ethical ordering of society matters of individual opinion. As such, they may very well influence the "inputs" of this or that individual to the operation of the political system, but they cannot set the goals of that system itself. Under these circumstances the only meaning that the elaboration of a political philosophy can have is that of unpacking and exhibiting one's own moral beliefs, and this does not provide a very strong motive when all hope of demonstrating any kind of suprapersonal validity for one's ideas has disappeared. On the other hand, while substantive ethical issues have been accorded this subjective status, other questions of a more formal kind have increasingly claimed the attention of political scientists.[12] These are typically questions about the rules that are to govern the activities of individuals in their participation in collective decision-making. Here the influence of conceptions of collective behavior which have been borrowed from economics has grown steadily greater, and the political system is now often understood by analogy with the market as a rule-governed procedure for arriving at social choices on the basis of the preferences of the individuals who compose it. As in the case of the market, these individuals are assumed to be more or less selfishly motivated, and the question is to determine what set of decision-making rules it would be rational for everyone to accept. Various versions of such sets of rules have been produced, and some of them—the 'one man, one vote' rule, for example—closely resemble moral principles of a very general kind. Nevertheless, the intent of most contributors to this literature seems to reflect greater interest in the simulation of the actual operation of democratic political institutions than in claiming any privileged normative status for the rules they propose. What is involved is at most a more intricate calculus of individual advantage, and it sometimes turns out that forms of political behavior

---

[12]For an overview of these developments in political science, see David Easton, *The Political System: An Inquiry into the State of Political Science*, 2nd ed. (New York: Knopf, 1971).

that have been condemned in traditional democratic theory—log-rolling, for example—are not only permitted by the proposed logic of collective action but positively conducive to the goals it seeks to achieve. In those cases, it is the traditional "idealistic" democratic theory with its expectations of a high degree of moral motivation on the part of the citizen that must yield to a more realistic appreciation of the logic of democratic institutions. In this connection, one is tempted to suggest that in modeling its theoretical constructions increasingly on those of economics, political science has been influenced more by classical economics with its conception of a self-regulating market that relieves individual entrepreneurs of the necessity of considering anyone else's interest, than it has been by Keynesian economics, in which the need is recognized for intervention directly motivated by a concern for the public interest. If so, one may wonder whether the fate of this new conception of a political "hidden hand" will be happier than that of its economic predecessor.

Because economics as the most technically advanced of the social sciences seems likely to influence the latter increasingly by its example, a word about the status of ethical issues within that discipline may be in order. While classical economic theory since Adam Smith had in some sense been built on moral foundations, the latter were of such a character as to insulate the economic sphere from political intervention motivated by moral judgments on the outcomes of unregulated economic activity. From the ethical standpoint, the most significant event in twentieth-century economics has been the massive and generally victorious assault of J. M. Keynes and his associates on the postulates of classical economics by which the immunity of economic activity from evaluation in ethical terms had been justified.[13] The effect of the Keynesian revolution has been to restore validity to moral questions about the operation of the economic system and thus to prepare the way for political intervention designed to achieve morally desirable economic outcomes. In a real sense, these developments in economics are comparable to those noted in the case of jurisprudence. In both cases the independence of a body of principles for the regulation of human conduct from external moral judgment has been challenged, and questions have been raised about the principles by which judgments of value in economics and the law are to be guided. In the case of the law, this led to a renewal of interest in natural law; in economics it has stimulated the development of what is called welfare economics.

---

[13]Keynes' major work is *The General Theory of Employment, Interest, and Money* (London: MacMillan and Son, 1936). A similar presentation of Keynes' views can be found in Robert L. Heilbroner, *The Worldly Philosophers*, 3rd ed. (New York: Simon and Schuster, 1967), Chapter 8.

The originality of the classical economists consisted in arguing that the economic activity of selfishly motivated persons would lead, under minimum restraints, such as those guaranteeing the sanctity of contracts, to the greatest possible well-being for all. So long as individual men are free to employ their capital and sell their labor where and when they judge the greatest benefit will accrue to them, the self-regulation of the market can be counted upon to achieve an optimal totality of satisfactions without any one being required to aim at anything except his own share in that total quantum of happiness. The Keynesian critique of these assumptions of the classical economists is too complex and technical for summary here, but its general import is clear enough. Primarily, it seeks to undermine the conception of a self-regulating equilibrium in the economic system on which classical arguments against state intervention had been based. Those arguments had always had a strongly ideological cast, since the equilibrium position was defined as the balance of prices and costs or of interest and profits that would be reached "if the general condition of life were stationary for a run of time long enough to enable all the economic forces to work out their full effect";[14] and in the real world that period may be indefinitely long. In the meantime, questions arise about private decisions to save and to invest and about the distribution of benefits through the population as a whole. Keynes argued that in fact these decisions were being made in a way that might satisfy the standard of private prudence, but certainly not that of any wider social good. It followed that the interests of different classes in society—the working class and the entrepreneurs—are really and not just apparently in conflict with one another and that there is a strong case to be made for centrally initiated action to raise the level of resource use and output and thus of employment. But the specific advice that Keynes gave with respect to the forms government intervention should take was less important in the long run than the fact that, as one of his collaborators has put it, he brought "the problem of choice and judgment" back into economics.[15] This was of course to bring back the moral problem as well, if only because the grounds for dismissing it or for supposing that it would somehow take care of itself had been shown to be invalid. Keynes did not pose as a moralist and certainly did not think that the state should try to supplant private enterprise or that it should in general substitute its own order of priorities for those that emerge from the operation of the market. Nevertheless, even temporary

---

[14]Quoted in John Robinson, *Economic Philosophy* (Chicago: Aldine Press, 1962), p. 84, from A. Marshall, *The Principles of Economics*, 8th ed. (London: MacMillan, 1920).
[15]Robinson, *op. cit.*, p. 8.

and remedial action by the state on the economic system reopened at the public level a host of questions that most economists had consigned to the domain of private choice, where each person within the limits of his means would have to answer them for himself.

The effort of economists to meet these new ethical responsibilities of their discipline have taken quite different forms. Some, like Professor Galbraith, and in the pre-Keynesian era, Thorstein Veblen, have assumed the standpoint of the practising moralist and have critcized the operation of the economic system and of the governmental agencies which supervise it from a point of view that is not in any formal sense ethical, but incorporates notions like that of the "quality of life" for which ethical warrant is evidently assumed.[16] Nevertheless, an antipathy for such ambitious enlargements of their professional responsibilities is still common among economists, and a more acceptable alternative for many has been the working out of a general theory of welfare on which specific judgments of the economic system and specific decisions to intervene could be based. "Welfare economics" in this sense has become a formidably technical discipline in itself, and it is not easy to summarize its ethically relevant aspects.[17] Although it is a lineal descendant of utilitarianism, it has significantly modified the utilitarian conception of happiness as a maximum of pleasurable feeling. Instead of conceiving happiness as a measurable quantum of pleasure, welfare economists treat it as a matter of ordering one's preferences for certain combinations of benefits in such a manner that a movement from one such combination to another counts as an increase or decrease in well-being. A state of well-being or happiness will then be one of occupying one's position of choice and being allocated the combination of goods to which one has given first preference. In this way all the difficult questions about the internal states of enjoyment produced by consuming various goods and services can be bypassed in favor of an objective criterion provided by the individual's own declared preferences. Needless to say, there are no ethical restrictions on the kinds of choices that can be included in this schedule of preferences. The problem the welfare economist then seeks to solve is that of constructing what is called a social welfare function out of these individual preference schedules—that is, a rule that will permit one to say whether one situation produces greater economic welfare than

---

[16]J. K. Galbraith, *The Affluent Society* (Boston: Houghton Mifflin, 1958) and *The New Industrial State* (Boston: Houghton Mifflin, 1971); and Thorstein Veblen, *The Theory of the Leisure Class* (New York: Modern Library, 1934) and *The Engineers and the Price System* (New York: Huebsch, 1921).

[17]For a review and critique of welfare economics, see I. M. D. Little, *A Critique of Welfare Economics*, 2nd ed. (Oxford: Clarendon Press, 1957).

another. In constructing this function, economists have generally denied themselves the right to make "interpersonal comparisons of utility—to say, for example, that x is happier than y or that x's satisfactions are more intense than y's—because this would in their eyes be tantamount to a judgment of value. Of course, simply by treating each individual's schedule of preferences as an element in the aggregate welfare of his society and by thus seeking to put him in the position of his choosing, an ethical commitment of a fundamental kind is unavoidably made; and more generally a theory of welfare that had no ethical content would seem to be not very much more than a technical exercise. Even at the purely technical level the attempt to construct a working conception of the social good out of individual preferences faces grave difficulties, as has been shown by the work of Professor K. J. Arrow, who appears to conclude that some "imposition" of preferences is required if a social welfare function free from internal paradoxes is to be constructed.[18] The impression the outsider takes away from the critiques of welfare economics by some of its expert practitioners is that practical implications are generated by its analyses only in the context of quite substantial independent ethical presuppositions.

II

Both sociology and anthropology emerged as distinct fields of inquiry in the course of the nineteenth century; for some time, especially in Europe, they remained more or less closely associated with their parent subject, philosophy. In the twentieth century, however, they have become fully independent and have developed their own principles of method for dealing with moral phenomena for which no special philosophical warrant is felt to be required. In large part, this was due to the work of the great sociologists of the turn of the century, notably Max Weber, Emile Durkheim, and Vilfredo Pareto who elaborated what were to become the dominant conceptions of scientific method in sociology. I propose to examine Weber's views with respect to the status of values as objects of scientific inquiry and as elements in the orientation of the social scientist. Then, shifting from methodological issues to the substance of social theory, I will take up the concept of society as a value system. In the widely influential version that is developed in the writings of Professor Talcott Parsons, this notion involves an interpretation of the moral role of the individual which seems to me to underlie a great deal of work in the social sciences and can therefore serve to pull together what would

---

[18]K. J. Arrow, *Social Choice and Individual Values* (New York: Wiley, 1963).

otherwise have to be a wide-ranging survey of a great many different conceptions of values as social phenomena. As it is, I will have to pass over much that is unquestionably relevant to our theme; and I can only hope that my discussion of the two themes that I have chosen—the one methodological and the other substantive—will compensate for these omissions.

At the end of the nineteenth century, the French sociologist, Emile Durkheim, made it a fundamental rule of sociological method that moral phenomena were to be treated and studied as "things"; and much subsequent sociological thought has been devoted to working out the implications of this requirement.[19] The first and most obvious such implication is that what the social scientist is to treat as a fact for his purposes must never be something that is itself expressed in value terms. It is only as believed or postulated or somehow entertained by some human being or community of human beings that values come to constitute verifiable states of affairs in the empirical world to which the social scientist is confined. This way of delimiting what is to count as a social fact typically reflects, as it did in Durkheim's case, an acceptance of the rigid positivistic distinction between the "is" and the "ought." If a science of human society is to define its objects in such a way that its assertions about them will be rigorously verifiable, then it must transform every "ought" that is implicit in the human attitudes and actions with which it deals into an "is." It can do this only if the facts the social scientist recognizes are cast in a purely descriptive mode and state only what some person or persons believe to be right or wrong and not what *is* right or wrong. In other words, from the standpoint of the social scientist, it is just a fact that human beings make certain judgments of good and bad and hold certain evaluative attitudes which they express in joint and individual actions of various kinds. These attitudes may be universally shared or highly idiosyncratic; they may be justified by rational or religious means or they may express the sovereign whim of an individual. All are grist for the social scientist's mill, but only as new or different facts and never as claims that he undertakes to certify or disallow.

No social scientist has defended this conception of objectivity with greater skill and consistency than did Max Weber; and many of his critical essays are exercises in detecting the innumerable ways in which the economists and historians of his day violated the distinction between a scientific and a normative treatment of value phenomena.[20] His discus-

---

[19]Emile Durkheim, *The Rules of Sociological Method*, 8th ed., trans. S. A. Solovay and J. H. Mueller (New York: Free Press, 1938).

[20]H. Gerth and C. Wright Mills, eds., *From Max Weber: Essays in Sociology* (New York: Oxford University Press, 1946) and E. Shils and H. Finch, eds., *Max Weber on the Methodology of the Social Sciences* (Glencoe, Ill.: Free Press, 1949).

sion of these matters is all the more interesting because he was fully aware that the practice of social science is itself a human activity and that as such it implies certain interests and criteria of value on the part of the inquirer which are in turn reflected in the choice of certain social phenomena or periods for investigation. He was also convinced that the object of sociological inquiry is social action which is meaningful for the agent in the sense of being a purposeful effort to bring about certain desired ends through the application of means that are thought to be appropriate to that purpose. But in the last analysis, for Weber, neither the values of the actual human agents that sociology studies nor the values of the sociologist that guide his selection of the objects of social inquiry can claim to be more than the subjective preferences of the one and the other. Social science cannot endorse or condemn the ideals it studies, nor can it provide solutions to the practical problems of men on the basis of the relationships it discovers within the domain of social action. What it can show is merely that a given action or type of action is consistent or rational from the standpoint of an assumed set of priorities or values; and it can do this because it has learned something about social causation—i.e., about the effects that actions of various kinds are likely to produce in the behavior of other human beings. When the social scientist makes a recommendation for social policy that is not cast in this hypothetical or, as Weber calls it, technical mode, he cannot claim the authority of his science for anything beyond the assumptions of fact and of causal interdependence on which his proposals rest. Weber did not believe that a social scientist or any other man could avoid making such decisions that bear on the most important issues of individual and social life; but he was equally sure that they represent personal acts which are arbitrary in the sense of being underivable from any factual premises and are made on the sole responsibility of the individual himself.

There is something very impressive about Weber's way of combining a commitment to a rigorous standard of impersonal scientific objectivity with a conviction of the unavoidability of choice; and one feels that this heroic ethic of personal responsibility is particularly appropriate in the analyst of Calvinism. In this connection, it should be noted that although Weber was utterly sceptical about the possibility of supplying any sort of cognitive warrant for value attitudes, whether those of the sociological inquirer or those of the individuals and societies to which inquiries are addressed, he does not appear ever to have been disposed to deny that these attitudes have great and indeed central importance both for the design of social inquiry and for the understanding of human action and institutions. He was committed to the view that explanation in the social sciences is finally causal in nature, but his own sociological practice reveals a predominant interest in interpreting the purposive and teleological structure of human action. Even the most obviously non-empirical beliefs and above all, religious beliefs, could, in his view, play an important causative role in such developments as the emergence of modern capitalism; and quite generally one senses that Weber's deepest interests were reserved for those constellations of meaning by which human life is ordered and given value. The fact, moreover, that these orderings cannot themselves be evaluated in terms of any absolute criterion did not stand in the way of understanding them and the actions in which they are reflected, in the way they are understood by the agents themselves. Weber followed common German philosophical practice in calling this reading of the subjective meaning of purposive human action *Verstehen*; but he was convinced that it was perfectly consistent with an acceptance of the canons of rigorous scientific procedure. By virtue of this strong emphasis on the value structure of the societies he studied as well as his insistence on the personal responsibility of the scientific inquirer for the choices implicit in his selection of research topics and the character of the interest he brings to the phenomena he studies, Weber's thought remains deeply imbued with ethical concern.

At least two kinds of considerations were to dispose many social scientists who accepted Weber's view of the subjectivity of value judgments against his predominant interest in those aspects of social life in which the role of value ideas is most conspicuous. One of these was a sceptical view of *Verstehen* itself and of the possibility of gaining reliable knowledge of the agent's perspective on his own actions; and to this scepticism behavioristic trends in psychology made a substantial contribution. The other was a tendency to throw normative beliefs into a common category of "nonlogical" beliefs together with all manner of myths and pseudoscience, in the manner of Pareto, without any of the fine discriminations or independent interest in ethical matters that were so characteristic of Weber. Once this has been done and an inevitably pejorative contrast has been implied between belief structures that are "logical" in the sense of satisfying the standards of scientific method and those "non-logical" ones, including ethical beliefs that do not, there is an almost irresistible tendency to conclude that the actions and beliefs that fall into the "non-logical" category have a kind of epiphenomenal character and should be interpreted and explained by reference to those in the "logical" category. The latter in turn are quite naturally associated with the satisfaction of those needs that collectively constitute the physical and the "economic" determinants of human action. In this way, the contrast between the "logical" and "nonlogical" becomes a contrast between, on the one hand, concrete human interests and the realistic adaptation of means to ends by which these interests are served, and on the other, those symbolic accompaniments that have to be understood, not in their own terms, but as somehow derivative from and expressive of the true and realistic interests that motivate human action. The introduction of this distinction marks a clear step beyond Weber's interpretation of normative belief systems, and the concept of "ideology" as applied to such systems carries precisely that implication of secondary and derivative status which Weber avoided and which is in fact quite distinct from the subjectivity he imputed to value judgments. Since the concept of ideology has in one form or another been widely used by social scientists and since its impact on the way they conceive ethical matters has been considerable, it deserves some discussion in its own right.

The term itself has a long and interesting history, but the sense it bears at present stems principally from Karl Marx.[21] For Marx the religious, moral, and philosophical beliefs of the dominant class in any society based on distinctions of social class represent a form of what he called "false consciousness." Certain standards and ideals and certain assumptions about the nature of man, which in fact only formulate and ratify the interests of a particular class at a certain stage in the economic and social development of a society, are promulgated as truths of universal validity and application. Their function is to reassure members of the dominant class by justifying their privileged position as being required in the interest of all men; to the extent that these beliefs gain acceptance among people who are not so privileged, they block and frustrate the efforts that might otherwise be made to construct a competing rationale of society calling for a redistribution of power and resources. The important point to note here, however, is that if Marx held that every society based on class antagonism generates a false consciousness or "ideology," he also looked forward to the advent of a society in which this ideological consciousness would disappear together with the antagonistic ordering of human relationship which it both conceals and supports. I have already noted that, for his own reasons, Marx was unwilling to describe the relationships of men to one another in such a non-exploitative and non-ideological society in moral terms, although many of his interpreters have argued that in this respect Marx's thought has a significant, if unrecognized, moral component. In any case, as Marx uses the term "ideology," it incorporates a contrast with an ordering of human relationships that would not be simply another fraudulent and unstable rationalization of the privileges of a dominant class; and while this alternative ordering had to wait upon the historical process itself for its effective realization, the strong pejorative connotations of "ideology"

---

[21]An excellent discussion of the history of the concept of ideology, including Marx, can be found in Hans Barth, *Wahrheit und Ideology*, 2nd ed. (Erlenbach-Zurich: Rentsch, 1961).

—the term we use to characterize the still prevailing theory of society—are really intelligible only against the background of this implied contrast.

Now what appears to have happened since Marx's day is that this implication of a contrast with an interpretation of human relationships that would be normative but non-ideological has steadily weakened until a point has been reached at which all social ideals and all normative conceptions of social reality are now ipso facto "ideologies." In a way, Marx himself may have been partially responsible for this development, since his unwillingness to say anything about the moral and rational justification of the classless society of the future made it appear by default that its sole justification lay in the class interests of the proletariat, which is a universal class only in a de facto sense, and might therefore plausibly be regarded as having its "ideology" like any other interest group. In any case, the paradoxical fact is that the term "ideology" has come to be assigned a universal range of application without losing the negative connotations that were originally dependent upon a contrast that is now no longer made. To be sure, one often hears statements to the effect that everyone has his own ideology tucked away somewhere or, as we say, his "bias"; and by this it is apparently meant that everyone has some beliefs about how society should ideally be ordered and that these very likely have some connection with or effect upon his scientific practice. But once again the unmistakable implication is that one should be rather apologetic about introducing such beliefs into general discussion. It is assumed that in the nature of the case these views can only be subjective preferences and, as such, mark lapses from proper scientific objectivity. Clearly, speaking of "bias" in this way makes sense only if we have some shared conception of what would in some relevant sense constitute "non-biased" views; but the notion that there are any available canons of criticism by which such distinctions could be made is one that meets with little acceptance and a great deal of scepticism.

The general effect of this indiscriminate use of the concept of ideology is clearly to demote all "non-logical" belief systems, including ethical beliefs, to a substantially lower status among the possible objects of sociological inquiry. It is also to treat the value context of social inquiry principally, if not exclusively, as a subjective source of cognitive distortion. It was, of course, so regarded by Weber himself; but he placed equal, if not greater, emphasis on the unelimizability of the value components in inquiry and that not just in a negative sense but as creating a deep ethical responsibility for the inquirer. Although many social scientists would agree with Weber that their research perspectives will inevitably be informed by value judgments of one kind or another, and that these should therefore be recognized and openly avowed, they appear to call for such disclosure primarily as a way of assisting others to discount the influence of such judgments on the research outcomes that are presented. Instead of a fuller and more conscious integration of scientific inquiry with the value perspective that inspires it, their goal seems to be an asymptotic approach to a truly objective social science through the progressive corrections which such avowals facilitate. Presumably, such a fully objective social science would formulate invariant relationships among abstractable features of social behavior which would be defined in value-neutral terms; and if the understanding of social processes that is thus realized were to lend itself to practical applications, then the ends of such application would have to be introduced from outside social science itself.

A portrait of the social scientist thus emerges which is very different from that limned by Weber and represents him as a kind of expert consultant or technologist engaged in what Professor Karl Popper has called "piecemeal social engineering." The latter "resembles physical engineering in regarding the ends as beyond the province of technology" and about ends all the social engineer can say "is whether or not they are compatible with one another or realizable."[22] But the ends which the social scientist cannot, under this self-denying ordinance, say anything about may very well be supplied by the sponsors of his research without any of his scruples about "ideology," and one significant consequence of those scruples will thus have been to disjoin the conduct of social inquiry itself from the responsibility for setting the value context within which it is to proceed. It is the latter of these tasks that has been most conspicuously neglected by social scientists in spite of the exhortations of sociologists like Robert Lynd and great research undertakings like those of Gunnar Myrdal in which a strong sense of moral direction shines through.[23] It is as though by accepting the discipline of scientific method with its rigorous exclusion of subjective preference from the determination of the truth, social scientists had disqualified themselves for a task that requires above all imagination, sensibility, and a sense of history. These are qualities of mind which the culture of the social scientist, divorced as it usually is from the humanities and resistant in principle to contact with "prescientific" ideas of the social world, is not designed to foster; and development by the social sciences of their own sometimes unnecessarily technical idiom of expression has not made things easier. Humane and ethical concerns have found it hard to keep their footing in a world of sociological constructs from which the dramatic character of

---

[22]Karl Popper, The Poverty of Historicism (Boston: Beacon Press, 1957), p. 64.
[23]Robert S. Lynd, Knowledge for What? (Princeton, N.J.: Princeton University Press, 1939); and Gunnar Myrdal, An American Dilemma (New York: Harper, 1944).

human life and action often seems to have been banished and in which even ordinary social perception—surely vital to any deployment of moral intelligence—is often impoverished rather than enriched by the conceptual spectacles it is required to use.

When one turns to the substance of social theory as distinct from these questions about method and the ethical stance of the inquirer, the underlying assumptions about ethics which we have been reviewing continue to exert a decisive influence. Quite often, as I have noted, the subsumption of ethics under ideology has had the effect of diverting sociological inquiry altogether from value phenomena as such; but even among those who retained Weber's strong interest in the latter, the doctrine of the subjectivity of values has significantly affected sociological practice in ways that might have surprised Weber. It is of course acknowledged by such sociologists that the value preferences of a given society cannot claim any more in the way of objective validity than can those of the social scientist himself; and that sociology as the scientific study of society can therefore do as little to vindicate or to criticize the values of the societies it considers as it can for the values that may be implicit in its own research agenda. There is, nevertheless, an interesting difference in the way the purely individual and subjective aspect of values is dealt with in the one case and in the other. As has already been noted, the value preferences or "biases" of the social scientist were, insofar as possible, to be discounted so that his behavior might be entirely consistent with the requirements of his professional role as a scientist. In the case of the individuals who make up the societies the sociologist studies, however, the ultimately arbitrary character of *their* value preferences has led many social scientists to concentrate their attention on the social roles a society recognizes and on the expectations and obligations that are associated with these roles. To these roles a measure of stability and objectivity—at least in the eyes of those who regard them as legitimate and binding on themselves—seems to attach; and it is not surprising that, as Ralf Dahrendorf has pointed out, sociology should have virtually subsumed individual human beings under the social roles they fill and that a *homo sociologicus* defined entirely in terms of these roles should thus have come into being as a successor to "economic man."[24] Necessarily, however, this strong emphasis on the way individuals receive their character and their values from the social roles they assume has had far-reaching implications for the way their moral functions are conceived.

These implications are very clearly manifested in the theory of a value

---

[24]Ralf Dahrendorf, "Homo Sociologicus," in *Essays in the Theory of Society* (Stanford, Cal.: Stanford University Press, 1968).

consensus that has been developed in the writings of Professor Talcott Parsons.[25] Here societies are viewed as action systems in which many human beings participate and in which the consistency and coordination of their actions is achieved through a shared set of evaluative standards. These standards apply to situations in which some human group faces alternatives among which it must choose *as* a group, and while the selection is always made by individuals, it must be made in accordance with some interindividual norm if it is to have any legitimacy in the eyes of others who may be affected by it or called upon to contribute to its implementation. Such norms express a "general moral consensus regarding rights and responsibilities"; and they specify certain roles or capacities in which different individuals act and to which more or less well-defined expectations based on the shared evaluative standards attach. Together with other standards—cognitive, affective, and so forth—these norms constitute the culture of a given society, and a premium is placed on "maximization of the consistency" of this cultural pattern. Indeed, it is not too much to say that on this interpretation the function of morality is precisely to integrate as fully as possible the action orientations of the constituent subgroups and of the individual human beings who compose a society. Morality is thus an expression of the fundamental need for order of human beings; and order here means primarily the absence of conflict and the harmonious complementarity of the activities of different individuals. Order in this sense can be realized only if the evaluative standards of the society are internalized by individuals "to a degree which will sufficiently integrate the goals of the person with the goals of the collectivity." Integration will, it is recognized, be achieved in different ways in different societies; but the possibility of unrestricted variations in respect of value orientations is rejected, as is the claim that every moral standard is somehow unique. Instead, an analysis of value systems in terms of a small number of "pattern variables" is proposed and differences among these systems are to be construed in terms of the possible combinations of such binary feature-pairs as universalism/particularism, achievement/ascription, affectivity/neutrality, self-orientation/collectivity orientation, specificity/diffusion, etc. Each of these features will, it is assumed, characterize the value orientation of a society to some degree and in some respects, and differences among societies will be those of the incidence and emphasis given to a particular "pattern variable."

---

[25]Talcott Parsons, *The Structure of Social Action*, 2nd ed. (Glencoe, Ill.: Free Press, 1949). I have also drawn on Parsons' contribution to T. Parsons, E. Shils, eds., *Toward a General Theory of Action* (Cambridge, Mass.: Harvard University Press, 1951).

What is most novel in this treatment of morality is the central importance that is attributed to its integrative function and the virtual silence
that is maintained as to other features often associated with morality.
Although it is recognized that only human beings are capable of motivation and that a value system must therefore gain acceptance from actual
human beings if it is to be realized, great emphasis is placed on the mal-
leability of the needs human beings must somehow satisfy if they are to
survive. The picture that emerges is thus one of the adjustment of the
internal economy of the individual to the requirements of role performance and generally of a maximization of value integration. No doubt,
such adjustments of individuals to social roles are required by all systems
of morality as they are by all systems of action. But if the requirements
of the latter are simply equated with those of the former, then some
paradoxical and perhaps unwelcome implications must be faced. Most
obviously, it will not be at all clear how an individual human being will
be able to make an independent moral judgment on the shared value
consensus of his own society or how such a judgment, if made, could be
more than an index of personal discontent and perhaps of incipient social disintegration and anomie. But especially since Kant and in very
marked degree in the course of this century, the claim that has been
made for the moral consciousness is precisely that it *can* criticize prevailing standards of personal and social conduct from an independent
standpoint and that it can apply to existing institutions and practices an
authoritative criterion of judgment, whether it be that of justice or of
utility or simply the indefeasible personal sovereignty of the individual.
If a moral judgment made in the name of some such principle is to be
simply treated as a counter-current within the dominant value consensus
and as a deviant bit of social mores, not only can there be no question of
its being able to claim any wider validity but—what is perhaps more dis-
turbing—it will very likely be subtly incorporated into the very ordering
of society it seeks to judge by being classified as a marginal resistance
to the prevailing value system. In Weber's theory of society, the potentially creative ethical role of the individual was recognized in his conception of the charismatic personality who alters the norms of his society
in some fundamental way; but this interpretation of the ethical life of a
society as a dialectic of the creation and the routinization of norms is
not easy to accommodate within the theory of value consensus.

An example may clarify the criticism I am proposing. There have been
many societies whose value orientation not only sanctioned slavery but
declared the only proper social role for many human beings to be that of
a slave. It is also a fact, however regrettable, that human beings can be
trained to internalize the requirements of that role to which many obligations attach but few, if any, rights. There is, in other words, no recog-

nition in such a value system of any fundamental relationship of reciprocity among all human beings. Now if we propose to categorize such a system as this as a moral code, and if we treat it as standing on a dead level with other codes in which slavery may be condemned and forbidden, then the only common feature of these conflicting systems will be that in one way or another they serve to integrate or organize in some consistent way the activity of some body of human beings. Morality as such will thus entail no limits on what may permissibly be done to other human beings. The professional posture of the sociologist in respect to these differences, among value consensuses, as to what is admissible in the relationships of human beings to one another, will be one of neutrality. While there is no justification for simply equating that professional neutrality with moral indifference, a legitimate criticism can be made on the grounds that this conception of the moral, which the sociologist finds it useful to employ in the course of his inquiries, is an extraordinarily emaciated one from which virtually all content other than the notion of "integration" has been evacuated. If the sociologist were ever to try to make use of it for normative purposes, it would prove a weak reed indeed; but a stronger and more fruitful conception of morality that *could* serve as an instrument of criticism and judgment is typically ruled out by his underlying value scepticism. Failing a stronger and more critical conception of moral judgment, the choice before him is therefore often one between a thoroughgoing abstention from moral judgment and an espousal of the value orientation of some group, whether orthodox or deviant, for which he knows no form of rational validation is available. The second of these alternatives is of course the one that is most often chosen; but quite often the social scientist who elects it seems to be rather self-consciously assuming an unfamiliar social "role" and there is something ventriloquistic and unconvincing about his performance in it.

The tendencies of thought I have been describing are those that have most strongly influenced work in the social sciences in this century and especially in the United States, where those sciences first achieved the scope and recognition they now enjoy. Nevertheless, these trends have not gone unchallenged by alternative conceptions of the methods and objectives of social science, and the critiques of this orthodox position by dissident sociologists have at least an indirect bearing on the ethical aspects of social scientific practice under discussion here. In one way or another, the focus of these critiques is on the nexus of the general social system and its shared value orientation with individual personality; and the claim they make is typically that this relationship is construed in a one-sided way which virtually identifies the individual with his social role. Perhaps the principal source of the views I have in mind has been the Institute for Social Research, which was founded in Frankfurt after the First World War. During the Nazi period many of its members came to the United States and the theoretical core of the recent social radical-ism may be said to have been inspired by their views, most notably in the version that has been widely disseminated by Herbert Marcuse.[26] The underlying assumption of this social philosophy is, of course, that relationships between classes are antagonistic in character; but in view of the fact—always difficult for Marxists to assimilate—that the stand-ard of living of the working class has steadily risen, it is not surprising that the forms of exploitation emphasized by writers like T. W. Adorno are primarily cultural.[27] Capitalist or bourgeois society in this late phase of its development is supported, so the argument runs, by the dissemi-nation, through education, popular culture, and the media, of an ideology which effectively short-circuits the development of any critical conscious-ness of the human situation under capitalism. So effectively is this ideol-ogy instilled that most people really accept its claim that a harmony of interests is being realized; and it is this "false consciousness" that the research techniques of contemporary social science take at face value. By doing so and by failing to understand that the opinions and attitudes it studies are themselves formed under the institutional pressures of capitalist society, social science not only fails in the critical task of de-mythologizing society, but also becomes itself an element in the institu-tional complex of capitalist society. Instead of depicting society as the deployment of a shared value orientation, social science should on this view be above all a critique of society's self-image and it should speak in behalf of the potentialities and interests of human beings that are mutilated or denied under present arrangements. To a considerable ex-tent, the dominant conception of this underlying human nature within the Frankfurt school has been Freudian in character; and that fact by itself virtually rules out the possibility that this critique might be formu-lated in explicitly ethical terms. Nevertheless, the critical role assigned to social science manifestly appeals to some conception of human self-realization which present social conditions block; and a social science that used such a conception as the basis for social criticism would be assuming an ethical role, whether acknowledged as such or not. Unfor-tunately, the style of this critique of contemporary society and culture is often pronouncedly élitist in flavor and seems to express the disdain of the European cultural Brahmin for the crudities of media-culture rather

---

[26]Herbert Marcuse, *Eros and Civilization* (Boston: Beacon Press, 1955).
[27]Adorno's work is known in this country mainly through his contribution to T. W. Adorno et al., *The Authoritarian Personality* (New York: Harper, 1950). His major work is *Negative Dialectic* (New York: Herder and Herder, 1971).

more than it does any genuine affinity with the interests of the less highly educated victims of ideological oppression.

Since I have been dealing with sociology almost exclusively up to this point and since the situation in anthropology as regards the treatment of ethical themes is somewhat different, a brief review of the relevant aspects of that discipline will complete this section. In the de facto division of labor prevailing between anthropology and sociology, anthropology has typically devoted itself to the study of non-Western societies and usually to the more "primitive" among these. It was natural that in the course of studying the mores of strange and remote peoples, attention should have focused on what appeared to be major deviations from accepted Western standards of morality. After all, the reporting of the mores and opinions of strange and remote peoples has been a favorite occupation of observers of the human scene from Herodotus to the present day, and the discovery that forms of conduct that are severely condemned in one's own country are permitted and even encouraged elsewhere has often stimulated a spirit of scepticism about the basis in "nature" of moral distinctions generally. Much of the ethnographic work of the nineteenth century appears to have been motivated by a similar interest in the sheer variety of ethical views that different societies exhibit; and in a book like Westermarck's *Ethical Relativism*, these differences supply the basis for an argument which purports to show that moral distinctions generally are expressions of non-rational preferences that differ from society to society.[28] The fact that the moral opinions held in different societies are incompatible with one another does not, of course, imply that none of them has any basis in reason or in nature; but in fact there have not been many thinkers who were willing to claim that many or most of the peoples of the earth were afflicted with moral blindness, as it seemed they would have to do in order to save the objectivity of moral distinctions in the face of the manifest conflicts of moral opinion which a wide acquaintance with human societies reveals. The doctrine of natural law was a theory of the basis in human reason of certain universally valid moral principles but, as its associated dictum *quod semper, quod ubique* indicates, it also involved a tacit assumption of the de facto acknowledgment of these principles by all human beings, however inconsistent their actual conduct might be with them. When de facto universality had to be given up, de iure universality was usually called into question as well. The alternative course of questioning

---

[28]E. A. Westermarck, *Ethical Relativity* (London: K. Paul, Trench, Trubner, 1932) and *The Origin and Development of Moral Ideas*, 2nd ed. (London: MacMillan, 1912–17).

whether such apparent differences of moral opinion really rest on ulti-mate and unresolvable moral disagreements among cultures was not to be seriously explored for some time.

For reasons that have already been reviewed, the notion of an objec-tive basis in reason for ethical distinctions has not been a live option for most social scientists in our time, and accordingly, the older Westmarck-ian kind of interest in the variations of moral opinion has grown much weaker, although in a work like Ruth Benedict's *Patterns of Culture* it is clearly still operative.[29] It is no longer simply assumed that differing sets of rules governing, for instance, the marriage of blood relatives neces-sarily reflect a basic moral conflict between the societies in question. Such comparisons presuppose that particular practices can be torn from the context of a given society and a more comprehensive body of rules and still be properly understood. Anthropologists have become increas-ingly unwilling to make that assumption and they have instead tried to understand better the place of a given rule or custom within the culture of the society that follows it, as well as its systematic interrelatedness with other rules of that same society. Very often this opposition to pre-mature external comparisons has made the mores of a given society something of a world unto itself, and this tendency has been strength-ened by the sympathy many anthropologists have felt for the cultures they have studied, as well as by an understandable resentment at the summary judgment of these societies as "primitive" which has so often been a prelude to exploitation and extermination. There is a real sense in which anthropologists, by undertaking the defense of the peoples and the cultures they study, have themselves assumed an ethical role. But if for these reasons and for others that have to do with a certain sensitivity and respect which anthropologists have often shown in their contacts with alien cultures, anthropology seems more permeable to ethical con-cerns than does sociology, this is true only with quite definite limitations, and does not seem to find much support from a consideration of at least two main sets of assumptions which anthropologists have made use of in the analysis of culture. Both have implications that make the rele-vance of ethical criticism highly problematic and leave very little place, if any, for an ethically motivated appraisal of a corpus of social rules, whether by members of the society in question or by outsiders.

One of these sets of assumptions goes by the name of *functionalism*, and was clearly formulated by Bronislaw Malinowski, among others.[30] It declares that every standardized social practice is functional for the

---

[29]Ruth Benedict, *Patterns of Culture* (Boston: Houghton Mifflin, 1934).

[30]For a discussion of functionalism, see Robert Merton, *Social Theory and Social Structure* (Glencoe, Ill.: Free Press, 1957), Chapter 1.

entire social system in which it is found. "Functional" in this use means, according to Clyde Kluckhohn, that the "bit of culture" so described is "adaptive from the standpoint of the society and adjustive from the standpoint of the individual."[31] In other words, it does a job within its social system which has to be done and for which this practice is uniquely suited. As Robert Merton has pointed out, functionalism was first developed by anthropologists who had been studying small preliterate societies which are in fact characterized by a very high degree of unity; and it was then generalized to apply to all societies. Even in larger and more complex societies, the functionalist admonition to assume that any established social practice makes a wider contribution has its value, since it may stimulate investigations in the course of which latent functions come to light. The crucial point of course is that this heuristic use of the concept of function must not be permitted to pass over to the status of an a priori truth. It must be itself subject to empirical testing in each case; and the possibility must remain open that a given practice has no substantial function or that it is in fact dysfunctional in certain respects. Unfortunately, these caveats have not been commonly observed. The word "functional" has an unmistakable approbative force which in effect shields the practice it describes from criticism; and when it is laid down in advance that all the established practices of a society are functional, a massive inhibition against criticism of the latter will in fact have been introduced. To criticize a social practice will under these circumstances appear as a failure of comprehension and as an improper application of external norms to practices which might well prove justifiable if assessed in terms of the value orientation of the society in which they are found. Quite clearly, if this line of argument is developed, there is a danger not only that any external evaluation will prove impossible but also that even within the society in question all actions, including those which at first sight might be thought to be violations of the local norms, will turn out to be functional, with the result that the distinctively normative force of whatever principles are recognized in that society will be lost and norms and conduct will be on a dead level with one another.

The functional position has been widely criticized along the lines followed here, and it now seems much less likely to exert the inhibiting influence I have imputed to it. To a considerable degree, its place has been taken by a new set of assumptions about the nature of society and the conduct of social inquiry which go under the name of *structuralism* and which in their quite different way seriously undercut the kind of autonomy that has been associated with the notion of moral agency.

---

[31]Merton, *op. cit.*, p. 26.

Especially in the work of the French anthropologist, Claude Levi-Strauss, an analogy is developed between language as a very complex structure of rules and kinship systems which serve here as a paradigm of social relationships generally; and emphasis is laid on the fact that in neither case need the individual human beings who use a language or intermarry in certain patterns know (in the sense of being able to state) the system of rules within which their speech acts and marriages take place.[32] In mapping these systems of rules, the linguist or the anthropologist is thus exploring a stratum of rule-governed action in which the rules are not necessarily consciously entertained or applied by those whose activities are governed by them. Levi-Strauss does not extend this form of analysis to moral rules as such, and he has on several occasions indicated that another form of analysis may be more appropriate for the study of advanced Western societies. But the rather clear implication of his position is that human beings enjoy only a very slim margin of freedom in relation to the system of rules within which they operate and which, he suggests, may themselves be laid down in the cerebral cortex. We can *tinker* with the structures of myth or of language, but in a way that is decisively constrained by the fact that the units which we rearrange have been formed within the original structural matrix itself and therefore can be recombined only in a limited number of ways. Applied to moral rules or codes of conduct generally, this view would clearly exclude revisionary choice or criticism at any radical level. It is this fact that has called forth Sartre's sharp attack on structuralism as an anti-historical denial of transcendence and the possibility of change. In some structuralists, views generally like those of Levi-Strauss have generated a markedly anti-humanistic rhetoric which in its more extreme forms celebrates the imminent demise of "man" in his role as demiurge of the moral and cultural world.

III

Psychology is in many respects as much a social science as any of those discussed in the preceding section, but I have chosen to treat it separately because the most interesting psychological work relating to ethical matters seems to me to have been done under intellectual auspices quite different from those of the social sciences which have just been reviewed. Sociology and anthropology are typically concerned with

---

[32]Claude Levi-Strauss, *Structural Anthropology,* trans. C. Jacobson and B. G. Schoepf (New York: Basic Books, 1963). For a good general review of structuralism, see Jean Piaget, *Structuralism,* trans. C. Maschler (New York: Basic Books, 1970).

the value systems through which the interests and efforts of many individual human beings are coordinated with one another; and these
sciences may be said to assume that human motives are such as to make
this socialization possible. The psychologist, by contrast, is much more
likely to be interested in the private motivational economy of the individual rather than its linkage to the larger social system; and his conception of the actuating motives of human conduct may set quite definite
limits to what human beings can do by way of regulating that conduct
by reference to moral principles. In some sense, therefore, the question
the psychologist asks is "How is morality possible?" and his answer to
this question must show how, in the light of some assumed theory of
human motivation, it is possible for us to comply with the requirements
of morality. In the older psychological literature, one often finds denials
that such motivation is possible at all as well as claims that "public virtues" are always traceable to "private vices"—i.e., to selfish motives in
the individual person. These older conceptions of human motivation as
necessarily egoistic in some narrow sense no longer command much acceptance among psychologists, but there is still a good deal of scepticism
as regards the influence on conduct that can be attributed to moral beliefs as such, especially when these involve some principle of a fairly
general or abstract kind. Accordingly, most psychological treatments of
morality have taken the form of efforts to show how the non-rational
energies of the self come to be mobilized behind moral interests so as
to provide the effective motive for the actions that morality requires. In
practice, this has meant that the cognitive dimension of morality has
been largely neglected by psychologists.

When one examines discussions of morality and moral development in
books on social psychology from the early years of the century such as,
for example, William McDougall's *Social Psychology*, one notes two
things.[33] First, the conception of morality itself that is presupposed by
the account given of moral development is pretty much that of common
sense; and while it does not transcend the framework of scientific nat-
uralism, neither does it attempt any significant reduction of moral ideas
into radically different or unfamiliar terms. Second, the emotions and
"sentiments" in terms of which the formation of moral dispositions is to
be understood are also by and large familiar ones: admiration, gratitude,
positive self-feeling, etc.—feelings which in complex interaction with one
another make it possible to develop the abstract and distinctively moral
sentiments such as love of justice and truth. But this way of dealing with
the acquisition of morality was to be profoundly altered by subsequent

---

[33]William McDougall, *An Introduction to Social Psychology*, 23rd ed. (London:
Methuen, 1963).

developments in psychological thought. Two major revisionary movements in psychology—psychoanalytic theory and behaviorism—changed in quite fundamental ways the terms in which the problem of moral psychology had been posed. Psychoanalytic theory did this by abstracting from the purposes and motives the human agent consciously formulates for his actions and moving to another level of analysis which is not that of physical behavior but of the unconscious teleology of human action and of the motives and feelings which, because they are largely unconscious, enter the conscious rationale of human action only in various symbolic disguises. Behaviorism takes the more radical step of throwing overboard the whole teleological vocabulary of both morality and the older psychology; and it seeks to understand all behavior, moral and otherwise, at the level of physical process in the manner of the natural sciences. In neither of these conceptualizations of moral phenomena do the cognitive or rational aspects of the latter figure in any significant way, and few, if any, questions are raised that reflect any sensitivity to whatever internal complexities the concept of morality may reveal. In what follows I will outline what I take to be the most important features of these doctrines in their bearing on moral questions. Then, because it contrasts so markedly with the general orientations in respect of morality of both these theories and because to omit it would be to give a very unfair picture of the present state of psychological thought, I will review briefly the cognitive psychology of moral development worked out by Jean Piaget. Although it cannot yet claim the degree of acceptance and influence that were earlier achieved by psychoanalytic theory and behaviorism, its star is currently in the ascendant and it is stimulating a great deal of inquiry and discussion.

While psychoanalytical theory has become a formidably abstract body of doctrine which seems to serve many of the purposes of a general *Weltanschauung*, its origins were in the clinical work of Sigmund Freud.[34] In the absence of a priori methodological inhibitions, Freud freely postulated the existence of various mental forces and entities as these were suggested by the exigencies of diagnosis and therapy; and the result was a complex stratified model of mental functioning in terms of which such phenomena as the acquisition of morality were to be understood. In this model the deepest stratum of human personality—the so-called "id"— is a set of biologically fixed instincts of libidinal drives with which each human being is endowed. These appetencies know no principle of limitation and no distinction between right and wrong. They demand satisfaction but they do not themselves comprise any understanding of the

---

[34]For an excellent discussion of the ethical aspects of Freud's thought, see Philip Rieff, *Freud: The Mind of the Moralist* (New York: Viking Press, 1959).

object realm within which that satisfaction has to be achieved. These instincts are thus blind both in relation to external objects and in relation to themselves. In due course, consciousness of external objects develops as a kind of outer membrane of the id to which Freud gave the name "ego." The ego is aware of external states of affairs in the way that the id is not, and can therefore perceive the dangers and opportunities they present for the satisfaction of instinctual drives. It accordingly assumes a kind of control over the otherwise chaotic instincts and determines the occasions for their gratification and their repression. It is the central executive agency of human personality and the seat of rationality; but its only regulative principle is the reality principle and its only function is to assure maximal gratification under the existing circumstances. Moral as distinct from prudential regulation of instinctual desires comes on the scene with the experience of other human beings and most notably one's parents, who set requirements for the conduct of the child that may be unrelated to, and often thwart, its impulses. Since these persons are more powerful than the child and can punish non-compliance with their standards, they present a danger to the id against which the ego must somehow protect it. But at the same time, the child's parents are in Freud's view themselves libidinal objects for the child; thus a painful tension of love and fear results. A resolution of this conflict is achieved by the child's internalizing the requirements that are initially imposed on him by his parents; and this development is described by Freud as the formation of a superego—i.e., a part of the ego which enforces, not prudential rules for the accommodation of our desires to existing opportunities for satisfaction, but "moral" rules defining what is permissible and what is prohibited conduct. The superego thus establishes a new and often much harsher control over the id; and while this control is most directly modeled on the superego of the parents, it is also an expression of the moral requirements of the society to which both parents and child belong and, in some sense, of all civilized human life.

On the basis of this theoretical interpretation of the multiple agencies that make up the self, Freud developed a therapeutic procedure for dealing with neurotic disorders. These are typically the result of a form of superego control which is too rigid and inflexible and which can be maintained only by the massive repression of the impulses and desires the superego will not permit to be satisfied. But in their repressed or unconscious state these desires continue to manifest themselves in indirect ways through fantasies, dreams, verbal slips, and so forth, and they generate a neurotic anxiety which threatens the integration and continued functioning of the self. Psychoanalysis is a method of intervening in such a situation for the purpose of bringing the unconscious sources of conflict to light, and for this purpose Freud developed a complex hermeneutic technique for reading the coded message of repression. It may be said to rest on three main assumptions. One is that even the most apparently irrational and fantastic episodes of conscious life are susceptible of an interpretation which relates them to a purposive strategy of the self and thus confers a certain rationality upon them. The second assumption is that this strategy is typically not known or accessible to the person in whose life it is at work, but must be grasped by the psychoanalyst, who then assists his patient to come to an understanding of the conflicts within himself. This self-understanding is the proximate goal of therapy and a necessary condition for the resolution of inner conflict. Finally, the origin of neurosis is assumed to lie in some disturbance of the patient's sexuality, and this disturbance in turn is traced to the latter's early life and to the character of his relationship to his parents.

In the popular imagination Freud has often been represented as a prophet of sexual liberation; and the goal of psychoanalytic therapy has been thought to be a dissolution of inhibitions and "frustrations" by which a joyous realization of sexual potentialities is blocked. These conceptions of Freud's treatment of sexuality are seriously mistaken. They quite fail to recognize that his principal concern was remedial—that is, to enable his patients to achieve something like satisfactory expression for their sexual and other needs—and that the underlying conception of normality in his work is much more conventional than it is licentious. Insofar as Freud had more general views about the role of sexuality in human life generally, they were rather sober and realistic; he clearly regarded the imposing of controls over the expression of sexuality as the price that has to be paid for civilization. It is true that in Freud's writings one gets a keen sense of the anguish that the imposition of social and moral rules occasions for the deeply narcissistic beings we all are; there have even been those who see in this very resistance to socialization and moral controls a creative and even an ethical principle. But Freud was not one of these, nor did he propose any general redesigning of the requirements of the superego that would make them minimally repressive. Indeed, one criticism that can be brought against him is that he was not critical *enough* in his implicit definitions of "normality," thus setting the seal of biological necessity on much that is culture-bound and presumptively remediable. But however that may be, it is not at this level of general social and moral principles that the ethical cutting edge of Freud's thought is to be found.

If Freud is not an ethical prophet, his conception of psychoanalytic theory nevertheless reflects assumptions of an implicitly ethical character. As Thomas Mann pointed out in his essay on Freud, one must distinguish between the picture of human nature that psychoanalysis presents and the use that is to be made of the knowledge of ourselves that we gain from it.[35] If that picture is a dark one in which illusion and blind desire dominate, it is also quite clearly Freud's conviction that such self-understanding can have a liberating effect. The premise on which psychoanalytic therapy proceeds is that self-knowledge, however painful, is a necessary condition for the overcoming of neurosis. There is in fact something uncompromising and stern in Freud's insistence that we must learn to accept ourselves and the world as they are. But if this amounts, as Philip Rieff suggests, to an "ethic of honesty," it is also an ethic of consciousness which requires that "everything pathogenic in the unconscious" be transferred into consciousness or, as Freud put it in a famous phrase, that "where the id was there the ego shall be."[36] What this suggests as a goal for therapy and for human maturation generally is an assumption of responsibility for oneself on the basis of achieved self-knowledge. As the contents of the unconscious are brought to consciousness, our relationship to them changes and our responsibility for them increases. Instead of being propelled by our unconscious desires as a kind of independent force, we will by recognizing them necessarily come to identify ourselves with them in quite a different way than was possible when these desires were acknowledged only in the disguises they were compelled to assume by our illusions about ourselves. In this sense, the movement that therapy seeks to induce is a movement toward moral self-ownership and toward a fuller assumption of the status of a moral agent.

Although these seem to be the plain implications of Freud's strong emphasis on honesty and self-knowledge, it must be admitted that Freud does not in fact acknowledge them and that there are features of his model of human nature which would make it very difficult for him to do so. To assign the responsibilities created by self-knowledge to "consciousness" is in terms of that model to assign them to the ego as the reality-oriented and managerial agency of the self. But within the Freudian system the ego has no independent source of energy and draws all its power to direct conduct from the id by a kind of trick that it plays on the latter. When a central executive role is assigned to the ego, however, then surely it must also assume revisionary and critical functions in relation to both the id and the superego, unless it is simply assumed that with the achievement of self-knowledge everything will somehow magically fall into place and inner conflicts disappear. There will be decisions to be made both about what requirements of the superego are to be

---

[35]Thomas Mann, "Freud and the Future," in *Essays of Three Decades*, trans. H. T. Lowe-Porter (New York: Knopf, 1947).

[36]Rieff, *op. cit.*, p. 104. Quoted from Freud's *Five Lectures on Psychoanalysis* in *The Complete Psychological Works of Sigmund Freud* (London: Hogarth, 1953), Vol. XI, p. 52.

treated as legitimate and which desires of the id are to be satisfied; and the making and carrying out of those decisions will require a great deal more "strength" than is available to the ego within Freud's system. A recognition of the problematic character of the moral life, even under conditions of achieved self-knowledge, as well as of the necessity for decisions of principle which that character entails, might have led Freud to reassess his treatment of the ego. If he had done so, there would still have remained another major obstacle, within his theory, to a fuller recognition of the moral functions of the ego. Here I have in mind Freud's construal of the relationship between analyst and patient within the psychoanalytic transaction.

As has often been noted, the relationship between the analyst and his patient, as Freud conceives it, is characterized by a marked absence of reciprocity. Due to the onesided cognitive authority of the former, it seems very unclear in what sense one can speak of collaboration between the patient and the analyst in the effort to understand and cure the former's emotional disorder. Apparently, the most valuable contribution the patient can make is to relax his powers of critical judgment, which are almost certain to be in the service of the pathological state in which he finds himself and can therefore be expected to offer resistance to the probings of the analyst rather than real cooperation. It is the analyst's criteria of significance that select certain items from among the patient's associations of ideas as significant, and it is the analyst's judgment, as that of the superior in a situation which "presupposes a superior and a subordinate," that interprets the condition of the patient and suggests perspectives for the reorientation of his emotional economy. Through "transference," or the emotional attachment of the patient to the analyst, the former is to be led to adopt the view of his condition that is proposed by the latter; and the expectation is that this interpretation will continue to be held by the patient beyond the term of his relationship with the analyst. One cannot, however, help feeling some doubt as to the survival power of a conviction that has been formed without the active and critical collaboration of the person whose conviction it is to be and under the essentially authoritarian tutelage of the analyst. As Philip Rieff has pointed out, it appears that with the sole exception of Freud himself, who carried out his own psychoanalysis, genuine self-knowledge will be possible only through the mediation of an analyst; and it follows that a permanent state of moral dependence upon others for the understanding of our own actions is unavoidable. In these circumstances it is hard to see how there can be any place within psychoanalytic theory for autonomy conceived as a condition in which one can perform these functions of interpretation and reorientation for oneself. But in that case it follows that the development of the ego toward a state of self-understanding and self-ownership and toward an assumption of responsibility for what was earlier imputed to the id or the superego will necessarily remain incomplete and the achievement of ethical maturity indefinitely postponed.

It can be argued, then, that from the ethical point of view the position of the analyst, in Freud's thought, remains privileged in a way that is not successfully accounted for. But if the analyst is endowed with a unique ethical authority, it becomes important to disengage the latent value assumptions that inform his work. In Freud's own practice, these assumptions were embedded in his theory of the stages through which human beings move toward maturity. In essence, this is a theory of the successive forms that sexuality assumes, beginning with "orality" and passing through anal fixations to mature "genitality." Each of these organ-references in fact designates a style of personality through which we normally pass but to which we may later regress. The ideal or "normal" course of development avoids such regression and achieves the stage of genitality, which for Freud connotes a full integrated deployment of libidinal energies upon appropriate objects, a confident and rather aggressive busyness with the work of the world and a freedom from the fears and avoidances that characterize the neurotic. David Riesman has pointed out that in many respects this rather too self-assertively "masculine" ideal of personality is culture-bound and may even mark the influence of Freud's own personal style upon his assumptions about "normality." Questions have also been raised about the implications of this ideal of personality for Freud's appraisal of the personality and social role of women in which a quite pronounced strain of biological determinism is manifested. Even Freud's emphasis on "genitality" has been attacked on the grounds that it subordinates sexual gratification in too restrictive a way to the requirements of a specific social role. The point to be made in all these cases is not that Freud was right or wrong, but that he was making tacit assumptions that had definite normative implications. Because these were not recognized for what they were, they were not available for critical assessment; and if an extraordinary man like Freud could be unaware of the normative elements in his own therapeutic practice, then others will surely not be immune to similar lapses. No doubt there are real limits on the degree of mutuality that is achievable within the therapeutic relationship; but at some point in the process, both analyst and patient must surely face normative questions more directly than present doctrine requires.

In light of Freud's lack of attention to the assumptions about normality that were implicit in his thought, it may seem surprising that the psychoanalytical movement should have developed beyond its original quasi-medical sphere of competence to become an all-encompassing interpretation of human life and civilization.[37] And yet this is what has happened; and in the course of this further evolution in which the so-called Freudian revisionists like Eric Fromm and others have been especially active, something like a popularized democratic version of psychoanalytic theory has come into being which proposes goals and offers practical counsel to a vast clientele. In general, representatives of this tendency do not share Freud's deep-seated pessimism about the permanence of tragic conflicts within human personality. Their perspective is melioristic and more directly moralistic than Freud ever thought of being; but their moral concerns are expressed in a psychological idiom that is borrowed with modifications from Freud. There is little or no concern with ethical principles as such or with questions about what kinds of actions are morally permissible. Instead ethical interest is concentrated upon one's own personality and upon the achievement of a certain personal orientation that is evidently judged to be desirable. This typically includes such attributes as "self-awareness" and "self-acceptance," "growth," "flexibility," and so forth. In the work of Erik Erikson, who is more hospitable to traditional ethical terminology than most of his colleagues, such attributes of personality are called "virtues" and a schedule of the acquisition of such virtues in the course of a lifetime is proposed. This psychological approach to ethical matters gives rise in its extreme form to what has been called the "mental health ethic"; and the latter appears to rest on the assumption that moral relationships among persons who have acquired the attitudes criterial for "mental health" will be unproblematic. Attention is therefore given primarily to the fostering of personality traits which will assure or at least greatly facilitate the resolution of such ethical issues as may arise, and notably to the elimination of rigidities of thought and conduct. In this version, psychological ethics coalesce with the American democratic ethos with its emphasis on flexibility and tolerance and its suspicion of commitments of principle it regards as dogmatic. This convergence has in fact made it possible for a psychological formulation of personal and moral ideals to become a kind of working ethic for certain sectors of American society such as public education. At the same time, social radicals and non-revisionist Freudians have not been slow to condemn these views as an ideology of conformism and of accommodation to the socio-political status quo. Whatever the justice of these charges may be, there can be no doubt that for many Americans the successor to the older conception of morality as a matter of rigidly defined rules of conduct has been a basically therapeutic attitude toward themselves and others.

---

[37]David Riesman, *Individualism Reconsidered and Other Essays* (Glencoe, Ill.: Free Press, 1954), p. 305 ff.

The doctrine that goes by the name of behaviorism is in a broad sense methodological in character and grows out of a strong sense of dissatisfaction with the results that are attainable when psychology is understood as the study of inner or mental states as distinct from behavior.[38] Because of the alleged unreliability of introspective reports of what goes on in people's minds and the further difficulty of understanding how such private events could be causally related to the physical behavior that is accessible to observation, the behaviorists propose a clean sweep of all references to such mental states and the designation of observable physical behavior as the sole subject matter of their science. Quite naturally this expulsion of the mental from psychology frequently becomes more than a methodological principle and emerges boldly as an ontological truth. When this happens, psychology is declared to have no subject matter other than behavior because there *is* nothing except behavior. References to inner states are treated as survivals of a pre-scientific world view on all fours with animistic interpretations of natural forces and the explanation of causal influence through the postulation of mysterious inner powers like Molière's famous "dormitive virtue." Needless to say, the Freudian concept of unconscious mind is just as objectionable to the behaviorists as the more familiar one of conscious mental activity; and they tend to regard psycho-analytic theory with marked disfavor on the grounds that it multiplies the number of mysterious and unobservable mental entities instead of reducing them all to the common footing of behavior.

The scientific work of most of the leading figures in the behavioristic movement has taken the form of experiments with animals under tightly controlled laboratory conditions. When studying rats in a maze, conjectures as to the inner states of the experimental subjects are necessarily quite limited; and yet it is claimed that without any reliance on mentalistic hypotheses very substantial success can be achieved in predicting how experimental animals will in fact behave under specified conditions. The same methods, it is argued, apply in principle to the much more complex behavior of human beings and can be expected to produce equally impressive results once the ghost of the inner mental state has been laid to rest. The functioning of the human organism must be studied as a unitary physical system, and linguistic behavior, instead of

---

[38]The pioneer in this field was John Watson, whose *Behaviorism*, rev. ed. (Chicago: University of Chicago Press, 1962) and *Behavior: An Introduction to Comparative Psychology* (New York: Rinehart and Winston, 1967) state the behaviorist thesis in uncompromising terms. Among the later and more sophisticated statements of behaviorism, one can cite C. L. Hull, *Principles of Behavior* (New York: Appleton-Century, 1943) and D. O. Hebb, *The Organization of Behavior* (New York: Wiley, 1949).

being treated as a report of mental goings-on that are outside that system, must be understood as a physical subsystem within the larger system of human behavior. That behavior is, moreover, to be explained solely by reference to biological endowment and environmental influence. All human behavior can be shown to be strictly dependent on these two factors, and there is absolutely no sense in which human beings can be said to be any more free in relation to the causal determinants of their behavior than a rat or a planet is. It follows that the whole picture of man as an autonomous being who is at least partly independent of the comprehensive system of causal determinism and determines his own behavior through free choices, is a fantastic one. Insofar as any such inner deliberative and volitional activity is discoverable at all, it has quite literally to be understood in terms of processes *in* the organism and in the closest kind of dependence on environmental influences. To the degree that behavioristic psychology finds it scientifically profitable to attend to those behavioral and physiological processes which have been misdescribed as inner deliberation and choice, it does not accept them on their own terms, which are purposive and teleological, but in terms of their utility in forecasting overt molar behavior.

If deliberation and autonomous self-regulation are myths, so quite obviously is the whole conception of man as a moral agent who is capable of recognizing and acting on certain principles out of a sense of his obligations as a free and rational being. As artifacts of discourse, moral concepts of course survive; but their claim to constitute a distinct language for the appraisal of human action, with its own canons of intelligibility and its own forms of efficacy, is simply and unceremoniously dismissed. All ethical notions must, for the purposes of scientific psychology, be quite drastically reformulated in appropriate behavioristic terms. Thus in the parlance of Professor B. F. Skinner, to say that something is good is simply to say that it is a "positive reinforcer" and this in turn is to say that it acts upon us in such a way that we come back to it or repeat it.[39] Bad things are negative reinforcers—i.e., their effect on us is to make us avoid them in the future. It follows from this that to make a value judgment is simply to classify a thing in terms of its reinforcing effects, whether negative or positive; and such a judgment is not a deduction from the natural law or from the categorical imperative, but a statement of verifiable fact about the relationship between the thing in question and certain organisms. Beyond the primary reinforcers that owe their effect to our natural constitution, there are the artificial reinforcers that human

---

[39]B. F. Skinner, *The Behavior of Organisms* (New York: D. Appleton-Century, 1938), *Walden II* (New York: Macmillan, 1948), and *Beyond Freedom and Dignity* (New York: Knopf, 1971). I have drawn most heavily on the last of these.

beings who live together arrange to influence one another's behavior. The principal forms these assume are reward and punishment; and for each of these there are derivative symbolic equivalents which compose our vocabulary of moral appraisal. Typically, these socially contrived reinforcers are designed to produce behavior on the part of the individual which serves the interest of the group as a whole. Sometimes an individual may seem to act in the interest of some wider good in the absence of such external controls; when this happens he is given moral credit and his free and uncoerced compliance with moral norms is held to reflect the peculiar dignity of which man as an autonomous moral agent is capable. In reality, however, external controls are operating even in these cases although in a much less obvious way. For a behaviorist like Skinner, the notion that a person can choose to adopt or not to adopt a policy of action simply reveals our ignorance of the "contingencies of reinforcement" that are operating.

There would be nothing especially novel or original in these views if it were not for the fact that there is associated with them the prospect of a behavioral technology. Such technology would utilize the knowledge the behavioral sciences are acquiring of how various kinds of behavior can be generated; and it would do so for the purpose of reshaping human life and society. According to Professor Skinner the controls over behavior that have been favored by those who believe in the freedom and dignity of man have been mainly punitive and extremely inefficient. Their failure, together with the development of other, potentially dangerous controls over nature, has produced a situation in which the survival of the species is in doubt unless we are willing to use the knowledge at our disposal for the purpose of controlling human behavior. But before that can happen we must overcome the strong hostility to deliberate control of human behavior that is rooted in beliefs about the autonomy and uniqueness of man. In his *Walden II*, Skinner has described an imaginary community in which the principle of "operant conditioning" has been made the basis of community life and behavior is systematically controlled so as to produce a harmonious and cooperative society. *Walden II* is in fact only one, fairly mild manifestation of a strongly utopian strain of thought that is common among the technologists of behavior. Their conceptions of the new man who is to be brought into being vary widely and sometimes border on science fiction fantasy, but they all accord a place to the controllers of behavior that is comparable to that of Plato's philosopher-kings. And it is of course just the latters' use of the enormous power that these schemes assign to them that raises serious ethical questions—questions that are already acquiring immediacy as the prospect of control over genetic endowment becomes more realistic.

There can be no doubt about the seriousness of purpose behind the program advocated by Skinner; but it is somewhat astonishing that he fails to recognize its ethical character and to make his argument in its behalf in ethical terms. There is no recognition that different goals might be proposed by the would-be controllers and that these might impinge in significant ways on what the subjects of such control conceive to be their rights. Instead, survival and peace are put forward as self-evidently desirable objectives, although this surely cannot be on the grounds that they positively reinforce everyone. On the all-important question of the controls to which the controllers themselves are to be the subject, Skinner is virtually silent; and what he does say is scarcely reassuring. We are told that there is *always* a reciprocity between controller and controlled; but the example given is that of a scientist who is studying the behavior of a pigeon and is, according to Skinner, thereby subject to a control exerted by the pigeon. Admittedly, the pigeon's control over the scientist has no intentional aspect, but intention for Skinner is simply a matter of being affected by the consequences of one's own action, and apparently counts for little. One would normally expect not only that the reciprocity holding between a human controller and his human subjects would be intentional on both sides but also that it would take the form of an understanding as to the objectives of the control exercised and the interests that have to be respected by the controller. In particular, it is essential that the controller not be allowed to control the critical powers of those who are to monitor and evaluate his work. Otherwise, Skinner's dictum that "the problem is to design a world which will be liked not by people as they now are but by those who live in it" would sanction the establishment of controls over all independent sources of judgment and thus insure that the controllers would be proof against criticism.[40] Admittedly, the requirement that controllers abide by understandings with the controlled will tend to have a conservative effect and this may be galling to those whose sense of the urgency of the needed changes is paramount. But to suggest that we should be satisfied by the assurance that under all circumstances we will, like the pigeon, be controlling our controllers is really just to dismiss the ethical issue altogether.

It may be reassuring that in a democracy as Skinner tells us, "the controller is found among the controlled" and thus has a motive for restraint and reasonableness in the measures he proposes since he too will bear their consequences. Although Walden II does not seem to depict a democracy, Skinner appears to approve such an arrangement; but he scarcely does justice to its implications. The point is that "counter-controls" are not just additional elements in experimental design. They implement the mutuality between controller and controlled on which the

---

[40] Skinner, *Beyond Freedom and Dignity*, p. 164.

ethical justification for controls rests; and they must themselves be out-side the control of the controller. Such mutuality does not and cannot obtain between the pigeon and the scientist who studies its behavior; but it can between human beings and the expert practitioners—doctors for example—to whose ministrations the former submit themselves. Skinner appears to be unwilling to formulate these shared understand-ings since they cannot be stated in the only form in which he is prepared to accept them—that is, as statements about the potentiality of certain states of affairs for reinforcing human behavior in a positive or negative way. But a failure to acknowledge any moral limitations on the control-ler's effort to bring into being a new man makes it very likely that no limitations will be respected in practice. Whatever its failures, the "litera-ture of freedom and dignity," as Skinner describes it, at least attempted to lay down the moral ground rules that will permit a society to direct its own affairs and, if it so wishes, to redesign itself. If such rules are a brake on needed reforms, they are also a prophylactic against the moral inversion of which Skinner's behavioral technology offers such a pure example.

Both the psychoanalytic and the behavioristic interpretations of moral phenomena in effect dismiss the possibility that moral discourse may have its own canons of validity and that the cognitive dimension of moral experience may therefore be worth investigating in its own right. Although this devaluation of the moral point of view has set the tone for a great deal of psychological discussion of ethical themes in our time, it has not gone uncontested and there has been at least one major effort to understand the acquisition of morality in the context of a general theory of cognitive development. I have in mind the work of the Swiss psychologist, Jean Piaget, whose pioneering study, *The Moral Judgment of the Child*, opened up a field of inquiry into which until quite recently other psychologists have been slow to follow him.[41] In Piaget's theory of moral development there is a close parallelism with the stages of cog-nitive development generally, and in both cases the movement is one from what Piaget calls "egocentrism" to a stage at which the perspectives of others are incorporated into one's judgments about events and actions in a way that corrects the partiality and distortions of a single perspec-tive. In the ethical domain this is a movement toward a state of auton-omy in which individuals, as Piaget says, "place themselves in reciprocal relationships with each other without letting the laws of perspective resultant from this reciprocity destroy their individual points of view."

---

[41]Jean Piaget, *The Moral Judgment of the Child*, trans. M. Gabain, (Glencoe, Ill.: Free Press, 1932).

Such autonomy is achieved, according to Piaget, only after passing through the stage of moral realism in which the authority of moral notions is essentially connected with the superior position of the adults from whom they are learned. At this stage, children regard moral rules as incapable of being changed by those who are subject to them. In relationships with other children, ideas of reciprocity and of consent as the basis for the authority of rules are acquired; and when these are fully espoused by the individual instead of being enforced against him by others, a supra-individual form of authority in which the individual nevertheless has rights of co-determination is realized. Piaget calls this final stage of moral development "autonomy."

Piaget's theory is, of course, put forward as an empirically verifiable account of the way children actually reach moral maturity, and has to be evaluated accordingly. The question of the theory's adequacy cannot be considered here; but I should like to draw attention to certain of its features which clearly set it apart from the other psychological approaches to moral phenomena considered in this chapter. First, the terminal stage in Piaget's schedule of moral development is characterized in terms of the kinds of ethical judgments of which people become capable; and the logical pattern of these judgments has a clearly recognizable affinity to our ordinary understanding of morality as well as to familiar philosophical renderings of our moral notions. Second, moral judgment is understood as a successful rationalization of one aspect of our experience of the world rather than in terms of internal psychodynamics or reinforcement schedules. The effect of both these features is to establish a connection between the psychological and non-psychological aspects of moral phenomena and between the movement of the individual human being through successive stages in the development of a capacity for moral judgment and the system of moral relationships itself within which that individual eventually takes his place.

Unlike psychoanalysis and behaviorism, Piaget's approach to morality has yet to engender a program of action or a social philosophy in which the practical implications of his position are worked out. Perhaps this is due to the fact that Piaget is not proposing to undercut moral ideas themselves as our principal guides for action by replacing them with alternative forms of control, whether therapeutic or manipulative; and it may be that this recognition within psychology of the integrity of moral judgment as such will prove to be the most significant wider contribution of Piaget's work. It has been proposed that practical measures should be taken in the schools and elsewhere to stimulate the movement of children from one judgmental stage to another whether by introducing them to simple analyses and illustrations of ethical concepts or by other means. If such attempts prove at all successful, and more ambitious translations into practice of Piaget's ideas are undertaken, then it might be necessary to raise questions about some of the unspoken assumptions of the Piagetian system. One of these has to do with the relationship of moral judgment to action; and another with the limitations that may be imposed on the moral development of the individual by the degree of moral maturity that has been achieved by the society in which he lives. If the maturation of a capacity for moral judgment is not necessarily linked to corresponding dispositions to act, and if there are stages of moral development for societies as well as for individuals, with some societies very far from anything that could be called autonomy, then the stimulation of the developing capacity for moral judgment of the individual will not necessarily bear fruit in action or, if it did, that action might be substantially negated by the incongruence of its moral environment. Nevertheless, whatever its ambiguities and omissions as the basis for a wider social philosophy, Piaget's thought is certainly the most hospitable domicile that an interest in ethics has found within twentieth-century psychology.

IV

The dominant impression one carries away from even this brief review of the social sciences is that of the central influence exerted by a certain conception of scientific method. I have in mind the view that the sciences —social as well as natural—deal exclusively in intersubjectively verifiable facts and that from these facts no inferences can be validly made that lead to conclusions about what *ought* to be the case. In the natural sciences, the kind of self-restraint necessitated by this conception of objectivity had proved immensely beneficial; and it has seemed obvious to many that the social sciences could become sciences in the full and authentic sense only by accepting this same methodological rule of treating everything that falls within their purview simply as fact and of rigorously excluding evaluative intentions of every kind from their work. Even at this late date, there is no reason to question the importance or the validity of this conception of the objectivity that scientific inquiry requires. It is of the utmost importance to be able to distinguish between what one would like to be the case and what is actually the case and to be able to determine the latter in full independence of the former. But what follows from the fact that scientific inquiry requires this kind of distinction or from the fact that moral inference may not conform to the canons of inductive or deductive logic Surely not that moral discourse is somehow comprehensively extrarational nor that science considered as a human enterprise can dispense altogether with shared ethical assumptions. Even in the case of the natural sciences in which the object of inquiry—nature—is not itself a moral subject and where the only controlling rule therefore may appear to be that of instrumentality to human purposes, we are beginning to wonder whether that is enough. When a science studies human beings as the social sciences do and may significantly change their lives through the social undertakings that are based on its findings, the need for some reflective formulation of the moral ground rules and value priorities for such inquiry seems clear. And yet such has been the disabling effect of the fact-value dichotomy that many social scientists have regarded any such undertaking as per se unscientific and perhaps even as an essay in theology. It is as though the justified conviction that at certain points fact and value must be carefully disjoined were held to entail a denial that there may be other points at different levels of the scientific enterprise at which they may and perhaps must be more intimately associated with one another. Of course, to argue against this view and to urge that science as a collective human effort has inevitably a moral dimension which needs analysis and articulation does not solve all the questions raised by such a view at one stroke and some of these questions are very complex indeed, especially those having to do with the way such understandings when achieved could be institutionalized without a serious loss of free initiative for the individual inquirer. But these obstacles in the way of an ethical *prise de conscience* for the social sciences are of a quite different order from those which, on the grounds of methodology, rule out all such discussions *ab initio* as extrascientific; and while the former are, as noted, difficult, they should not prove unmanageable once crippling preconceptions are set aside.

Hello the world.
But why little about the
"humanities" in general

THREE

*ethics
and the
humanities*

Bad
on

The term "the humanities" does not have a completely stable denotation, but for the purposes of this book it will designate history and literature. Although philosophy would normally be comprised among the humanities, it has already been presented separately as a context for ethical thought. There are, in any case, good reasons for treating literature and history together and in isolation from philosophy. Both are concerned with the portrayal of human character and action and both have an interest in individual human beings which is quite different from the philosopher's. In limiting the humanities to history and literature I am also excluding the fine arts—music, painting, sculpture, and so forth—from the purview of this study. This is not, however, to imply that these arts have nothing to do with ethics. Not only is the artist's motivation often difficult to characterize without some reference to ethical themes, but the work itself may well portray scenes or express feelings that are at least implicitly ethical. Nevertheless, it is very hazardous and difficult to interpret the ethical content of works of art in a nonverbal medium;

and I, for one, lack the self-confidence of a Jean-Paul Sartre, who unhesitatingly associates a musical composition like the Well-Tempered Clavier with an abstruse theorem of ethical theory like Kant's categorical imperative. I will, therefore, confine myself to an examination of the relationship between ethical ideas and the accounts that are given of individual and social life in the history and in the imaginative literature of our time.

'Since the humanities are widely believed to have a special concern with, and are even supposed by many to discover and to teach, "values," it might seem that the informing influence of the latter on history and literature should be much more obvious than it is in the case of the social sciences. If these are our expectations, however, they may prove somewhat misleading. Whatever their degree of interest in values, most historians and most novelists and poets are quite sparing in the use of language that has a directly ethical import. Thus, even those historians who most strongly disapprove of someone like Hitler do not necessarily consider it to be their duty to pass an explicit moral judgment on his character and actions; and a good novelist is usually careful not to categorize too directly the moral quality of the motives of his protagonists. There is, in fact, something faintly incongruous in the very notion of either an historian or a novelist treating the human events, real or imaginary, which he has to recount as so many "cases" on which he can bring to bear an ethical calculus; if he were to do so, his ability to understand and to render the complexity of human motivation and character would be prima facie suspect. But if the moral concerns of historians and novelists do not normally take the form of declarative judgments, no one can seriously doubt that such concerns are very much at work in the design and elaboration of the accounts they give us of human events. They are typically present in mediated form and in association with other ideas of a less immediately moral nature. In the case of history these associated ideas are likely to be models or schemata of the historical process, while in imaginative literature they will often take the form of conceptions of human character or of the recurrent themes of human experience. It will be useful, therefore, to identify at least some of the schemata that have been used to organize historical and fictional narratives in our time and to try to define the ethical import they carry. In this way it may be possible to gain some insight into the character of the • ethical consciousness that has informed the historical thought and the imaginative literature of this century.

Although the relationship of the humanities to philosophy (or for that matter to the social sciences) has not been close or continuous, philosophical ideas have unquestionably had considerable impact on the treatment of ethical matters. If a single philosopher had to be named for his paramount influence upon the way humanists generally have conceived their enterprise, it would probably be Friedrich Nietzsche, although until recently that influence has been felt most strongly on the Continent and less so in the English-speaking world. The general character of his influence has already been defined, and its reflection in the imaginative literature of twentieth-century Germany has been brilliantly described by Eric Heller.[1] More generally, however, and apart from its specific derivation from Nietzsche, a certain set of assumptions about ethics has tended to form the common background of thought for a great many historians and writers of our time. Whether for good reasons or bad, it has come to be widely believed that the traditional justifications for the values, moral or otherwise, that are proposed for recognition and acceptance by individual human beings, do not pass the test of critical scrutiny, and that all values have thus become in a radical sense dependent upon acts of preference which may be in some final sense arbitrary. This demise of absolute values has been closely connected with analogous developments in the religious experience of our time—notably the so-called "death of God"—as well as with the disintegration of hierarchical social arrangements which often claimed to derive their validity from these ethical and religious beliefs of which they claimed to be the institutional counterpart. By some these changes were experienced as tragic and by others as liberating, but for all reflective historians and writers they raised serious questions about the authority they could claim for any particular ordering of the incidents of human life and history as these are displayed in the novels and dramas and histories they produce. Traditionally, that ordering had derived its authority from a set of conceptions of the common good, of personal virtues and of the goal of human history that were, in spite of much secularization, of Christian origin. While serious doubts about this ethical ordering of the personal and the public world had been expressed throughout the modern period, it was in the twentieth century that for the first time these doubts became the common ground of intellectual life. The result has been a crisis whose intensity can perhaps be measured best in the humanities, where the need for an ethical framework of acknowledged validity is most widely believed to exist. In this chapter, I hope to illustrate some of the ways in which the history and literature of our time have attempted to discharge their traditional functions under these new and difficult conditions.

At the same time as the ethical presuppositions on which humanists have traditionally relied were coming to seem more and more problematic, and to some extent for just that reason, attention was being drawn to the role such presuppositions play in the construction of the "stories" which the historian or the novelist tells. Increasingly, the business of recounting human events, whether real or fictional, appeared to the prac-

---

[1] Eric Heller, *The Disinherited Mind* (New York: Farrar, Straus and Cudahy, 1957).

titioners of history and literature to be anything but straightforward, and an element of subjectivity and partisanship came to be viewed as necessarily implicit in such activity.⟩Thus, a number of studies by practising historians of the nature of the historical enterprise itself have substantially refuted the positivistic supposition that history is exclusively concerned with "facts" and that history is "scientific" in proportion as it resolutely dispenses with theory. In place of this simplistic view, most historians now accept the importance of the terms in which their questions—the questions to which "facts" provide answers—are formulated and they recognize that these modes of conceptualizing their materials form part of a larger intellectual perspective within which a whole range of ethical questions may be subtly prejudged. Similarly, in the field of literature, there has been a marked increase in the attention paid to the point of view of the author, to the consciousness that carries the story, and to the implications various narrative devices have for the way events are envisaged and presented. Such modes of orientation reflected in the design of literary and historical works may be associated with a certain class position or with a certain type of culture; and when they are, their use will express a social *parti pris* on the part of the writer even though he seeks to be scrupulously careful and fair in his assessment of evidence. Such a priori elements in history and literature may not have a primarily ethical character, but they provide the criteria in terms of which distinctions are made between what is important and what is unimportant, what is relevant and what is not, and so on; and such determinations prepare the ground for explicit evaluative judgments. For such reasons as these, humanists, like social scientists, have increasingly found themselves in the position of having to recognize that their enterprise rests on ethical presuppositions at the same time as the epistemic credentials of ethical beliefs generally were being called into question. In these circumstances, it is hardly surprising that there has been a considerable displacement of the locus of ethical concern on the part of many novelists and historians, from the lives of the human beings about whom they write to the situation and the moral options of the writer himself.

I

Whatever inhibitions the contemporary historian may feel in connection with "value judgments," the moral vocation of history is of long standing; it finds apt if somewhat exaggerated expression in the dictum that history is philosophy teaching by example. In antiquity and well into the modern period, history was held to be the record of great deeds; and great deeds require great men. The purpose of history was to save these deeds from oblivion so that they and the character of their authors might serve as an example to succeeding generations and thus inspire emulation. Needless to say, the deeds of great men assumed their full value only through contrast with the failures and infamies of lesser men, and accordingly, historical narratives tended to be dominated by the chiaroscuro of strong dramatic contrasts between good and evil, nobility and villainy. Of course, the perspective from which such moralistic histories were written was usually more parochial than universal; in practice the measure of good and evil was defined by reference to the interests of Islam or Christendom, Florence or France—interests which were assumed to be self-evidently compatible, if not identical, with the requirements of whatever universal principle of morality the historian recognized. Viewed in this light, human history becomes a struggle between protagonists who represent moral forces which are themselves timeless and independent of the vicissitudes through which human societies as the bearers of such values pass.

This interest in the moral aspect of human events has typically found its most natural expression in political history. Political history traditionally deals with the making of policy and with the character and actions of the statesmen who make it. Men's lives are greatly affected for better or worse by such decisions, and it is understandable that the historian who relates the events in which these decisions often account for so much, should feel moved to appraise them in the light of what he knows about the circumstances in which they were made and the consequences to which they led. Sometimes this appraisal may be of a purely technical kind and concern only the actor's mastery of some special political skill. But more often the appraisal is cast in broader and less specialized terms and appeals to some assumed standard of what is wise or just or practical, by reference to which specific decisions, as well as the career and character of some central figure are then judged. Political historians in our time have unquestionably continued to make critical assessments of men and policies along these lines. As I have already noted, they tend, in making these assessments, to avoid directly moral language that portrays some men and their motives as morally bad in some unambiguous sense and others as morally good. In fact, however, the difference between a directly moral judgment and the less aggressive observations typically offered by twentieth-century historians is not always very substantial, especially when one remembers that such critical comments reflect a general political orientation which quite commonly does double duty as the historian's ethical *Weltanschauung*. This point has been admirably expressed by the late Professor Richard Hofstadter.

An interpretative judgment . . . is not exactly a moral judgment but it plainly provides part of the structural frame within which moral judgments are set. . . . While the historian does not have to set himself up as a moralizer, he is constantly dealing with the substantive setting within which moral judgments are made, constantly trying to provide a sense of the requirements and limitations of social situations, of the effects which actions and decisions have had on large numbers of people.[2]

In the historiography of the twentieth century, at least two such "structural frames" can be discerned within which politico-moral assumptions of a very general kind in effect organize the historical phenomena under study in a way that lays the groundwork for eventual evaluative judgments. One of these is that of national history, in which interest is focused on the development of the central institutions of government and upon the activity of the state as the prime historical agent in the field of both domestic and international affairs. The other, which has been characteristic of liberal historiography assumes a more detached and skeptical attitude toward the state and interprets the historical process in terms of the progress toward freedom and well-being of society as a whole and of the "people" who are often conceived to be in an adversarial relationship to the state. In its simplest terms, the difference between these two approaches is the difference between a strongly positive view of the national state as the bearer of civilization and of the higher ethical interests of man generally and a view that qualifies this attitude toward the state by reserving large areas of freedom to individuals and to institutions other than the state. Both conceive historical progress in primarily political terms, and in both liberal history and national history the dramatic and even personal character of the decisive episodes tends to be strongly emphasized.

In large part, the evolution of twentieth-century historiography is the record of the progressive qualification of the allegiance of historians to these politico-moral orientations. To some extent, these trends have been motivated by the movement of twentieth-century history itself, which has made it very difficult to assign a positive moral role to the national state or indeed to "the people." At the same time, doubts have arisen as to the epistemic value of politico-moral history of whatever description, especially as the development of the social sciences has suggested the applicability to history of new methods of analysis and the use of new kinds of evidence. In general, the tendency of these newer conceptions of historiographical method has been to assign a much reduced role to those elements in historical events to which moral interest has traditionally attached itself, and to give greater prominence to a stratum of events to which that interest can hardly find any natural relationship. There

---

[2]Richard Hofstadter, *The Progressive Historians* (New York: Vintage Books, 1970), p. 229.

have also been, as I will try to show, certain compensating aspects of these new movements in historiography through which the moral interest in history may find new avenues of expression. But for the most part the decay of the older conceptions of politico-moral history has been followed by the introduction of specialized and technical forms of historical analysis, which are either value-neutral or at least do not appear to have any clear implications for moral judgment on the events with which they deal.

A classical characterization of the liberal tradition of historiography can be found in Professor Herbert Butterfield's *The Whig Interpretation of History*.[3] This tradition is distinguished by a strong interest in the moral aspect of history, and it regards moral progress as consisting largely in the growth of religious and political freedom. Originally this conception of history was of Protestant inspiration, as is very noticeable in the writings of Macaulay, but the Catholic historian, Lord Acton, subscribed to a very similar view of the central position of freedom in history without the same religious prepossessions.[4] Associated with this moral approach to history is a belief in an essential continuity and identity of purpose among all the efforts that have been made across the centuries to expand and secure human freedom. Thus viewed, Luther and Charles James Fox stand in a single line of historical figures who have cumulatively achieved the measure of freedom we enjoy today; it is this line that gives direction and point to history as a morally significant and humanly interesting field of study. Of course, the continuity which is thus introduced into history is, in Butterfield's view, altogether too smooth and it often obscures the peculiarly dialectical character of the historical process by virtue of which its outcomes so often express the original intent of none of the contending parties but rather, as in the case of the religious toleration that emerged from the religious wars of the seventeenth century, something quite different that was accepted only because the original objectives proved unrealizable. Typically, liberal history tends to elide and foreshorten whatever elements in the past resist incorporation into the moral unities of the drama it is concerned to reenact. The protagonists in that drama have typically been, on the one hand, some political or religious institution which denies or restricts the freedom of the "people" and, on the other, those persons or groups who are assumed to represent and defend the interests of the society as a whole. This is not to say that liberal history must necessarily be hostile

---

[3] Herbert Butterfield, *The Whig Interpretation of History* (London: Bell and Sons, 1931).

[4] Lord Acton, *Essays on Freedom and Power*, Gertrude Himmelfarb, ed. (Boston: Beacon Press, 1948).

to the state or refuse it any role in the history of freedom, but it is likely to take a positive view of the state's contribution only if it defends the people against some alien or domestic oppressor and if it is suitably modest in defining its own powers of supervision and control.

In the early decades of this century, liberal history in the nineteenth-century manner was still very much alive and continued to set the dominant intellectual and moral tone for the historical profession in Western Europe and America. In its American manifestation it went under the name of "progressivism." Like the liberal, but in a somewhat more populistic spirit, the progressive historian views history as the struggle for freedom and well-being of the "people" against the selfish and repressive forces that control the economy and too often the state as well. Every political act that denies to the people the right to share fully and effectively in the direction of the policies and institutions that influence their lives must be condemned as inconsistent with democratic principles and, by implication, as morally indefensible. Political leaders who make themselves the champions of the interests of the people and remove the barriers to equal opportunity and advancement that have been established by privilege thereby qualify for approval on grounds that are at once political and moral. In the United States, the contrast between repression and liberty was often associated with the differences between Europe and America and between the eastern Europe-oriented part of the country and the newer more democratic West, which suffered under the economic domination of the East. Together, these assumptions provided the essential framework for a strongly partisan interpretation of American history, and it was this interpretation as developed by Charles Beard, F. J. Turner, and V. L. Parrington that was to dominate American historiography up to the Second World War. Like its counterparts in England and France, it found one of its centrally important inquiries in the revolution to which existing liberties were traced and in the constitution adopted in the years that followed. In what was to become one of the classic documents of the progressive historiographical tradition, Beard argued that the Constitution was inspired by the conservative political attitudes of the economically powerful groups in the colonies who wanted to contain the potentially dangerous tendencies of democracy. In the course of his analysis of the class and economic situation of the membership of the Constitutional Conventions, Beard again and again suggested that the founders were actuated by selfish personal and class interests which were directly opposed to the movement toward a truly popular democracy. But, as Professor Hofstadter has shown, Beard apparently did not recognize that, in the context of the broader political judgments he had made, his characterization of the motives of the sponsors of the Constitution amounted to a strongly adverse moral judgment

on them and on their policies.[5] This example illustrates the way historical judgments made within a political framework like the Progressivism
of Beard and Turner function in very much the same way as did the
openly moral conclusions of earlier historians. It has typically been in
this mediated fashion that the progressive or liberal tradition has enunci-
ated its moral estimates of the persons and events with which it has
dealt; and the writings of A. M. Schlesinger, Jr., especially his histories
of the Jackson, Roosevelt, and Kennedy administrations, offer a current
example of that reading of American history.[6]

The reasons for the movement of historians away from the progressive
or liberal conception of history are many, and prominent among them
was a growing sense of unresolved ambiguities in the ideology of liberalism. In the eyes of Marxists, liberalism has always been the perspective upon society and history of a particular class, the bourgeoisie; they
have not been slow to point out contradictions between the claim of liberalism to represent the interest of all classes and the dominant influence
of narrowly middle-class interests upon its programs and its conceptions
of social goals. But even among non-Marxists and historians trained in
the liberal tradition, there has developed in the course of this century a
strong sense of the ambiguities and ironies of the historical process and
a resulting unwillingness to accept uncritically the older Progressive co-
ordinates of political and moral evaluation. In part, this new reserve, at
least when it is not inspired by a lack of interest in moral issues as such,
reflects an understanding of the fallacies of the Whig interpretation of
history to which Professor Butterfield has drawn attention, and a rejection of such anachronistic imputations of moral continuity as those that
permitted the historian to celebrate Martin Luther as a pioneer of religious liberty. Related to this rejection of false continuities is a perception of how rarely historical actors can control the consequences of their
actions and how often morally desirable outcomes are traceable to causes
which from an ethical point of view are either neutral or negative in
character. Finally, the darkening moral atmosphere of the mid-twentieth
century, sometimes reinforced by the teachings of neo-orthodox theology, have induced a sense of the complexity and contradictoriness of
human character and thus of the inappropriateness of simplistic moral
appraisals in history.

Perhaps the best example of the work that has been influenced by this
sense of moral complexity is in the writings of Richard Hofstadter whose
treatment of the Progressive historians I have just been laying under
contribution. In his most important books—*The American Political Tra-*

---

[5]Hofstadter, *The Progressive Historians*, p. 229.
[6]A. M. Schlesinger, Jr., *The Age of Jackson* (Boston: Little, Brown & Co., 1945) and
The Age of Roosevelt (Boston: Houghton Mifflin, 1957).

dition and *The Age of Reform*—Hofstadter worked in an area that is intermediate between political ideas and political events; the result is critical history that infuses the portrayal of individual men with a sense of the idea or policy that gives their careers meaning. Hofstadter was sometimes regarded as a political conservative because he dealt rather astringently with some of the heroes of the liberal tradition, and it is certainly true that his judgments of men and issues were made in a more independent spirit than one usually associates with liberal history. It was, however, precisely through this capacity for detachment that Hofstadter was able to gain some of his most valuable insights into the ironies of history. These ironies, as often as not, turned on the fact that a movement of protest or reform was deeply implicated in the very system which it was ostensibly undertaking to change; as in the case of the Populists whom Hofstadter shows to have been, for all their sense of being the victims of capitalist exploitation, small-scale agrarian entrepreneurs themselves. In this case, as in the case of the Progressive movement as a whole, Hofstadter's method was to play off an individual's or movement's sense of what it was trying to achieve against his own independent interpretation of that achievement and while the implied criticism is not moral in the sense of condemning or justifying in some final sense those with whom it deals, it is certainly moral in that it expresses a priority of interest in what human beings, at the behest of certain needs and guided by certain ideas, try to make of themselves and their world.

For all his scepticism and his sense of the ironies of history, Hofstadter remained deeply interested in the human and moral dimensions of the historical process. A very much more radical break with the ideals of liberal historiography is made in the work of the English historian, E. H. Carr. His case is the more interesting because he has himself very clearly formulated the ideas about the historian's function which are illustrated in his own historical writings and especially in his *History of Soviet Russia*. In its most general terms, Carr's approach to the study of political phenomena rests on a fundamental contrast between "utopianism" and "realism." The former is a set of assumptions that reflect a primary interest in the way things *ought* to be and they tend to pass over into claims that what should morally be the case already in fact is so. By way of example, Carr points out that a great many statesmen and thinkers of the nineteenth and early twentieth century appeared to believe that a harmony of the interests of the different nations that compose the international community was, in fact, a reality, or at any rate would be as soon as more people had come to understand that their true interests

---

[7] E. H. Carr, *A History of Soviet Russia* (London: Macmillan, 1952).

could only be achieved through peaceful cooperation with other nations. Carr suggested that this doctrine of the harmony of interests was really a bit of ideology uniquely appropriate to the situation of the satisfied powers who wanted others to accept a dispensation which was in fact one-sidedly advantageous to its proponents. Thus, an ostensibly moral way of looking at the relationships between nations in practice often serves as a rationalization of selfish interests; but at the same time it induces a systematic tendency to underestimate the reality of power in the world—a tendency which has been especially characteristic of liberal statesmen and historians who were apparently taken in by their own rhetoric. The realist, by contrast, automatically discounts highflown idealism as a pretense and looks for the interested motive which underlies it and which alone, he assumes, can explain human conduct. He seeks to understand human behavior and the behavior of states simply as they are and not through the lens of some special moral requirement. In fact, at his most consistent, the realist rejects the very notion of moral judgment as such, especially in the case of states, and if he has any criterion for judging episodes in the historical process, it is simply the non-moral criterion of success—i.e., the capacity a statesman reveals for achieving what he sets out to do. To be sure, Carr regards a fully consistent realism as impossible and holds that all of us must be to some extent utopians. But this seems to mean that we cannot help embracing moral beliefs even though these necessarily involve an element of self-deception. An unavoidable coefficient of illusion is thus attributed to the moral attitude; and while it may sometimes seem that Carr is making a case only against certain exaggerated and absurd beliefs which have sometimes been associated with the moral perspective on political events, his deeper intention clearly makes this misrepresentation of reality the essence of the moral, with the result that no way is left of espousing the role of the moral critic that is not at the expense of one's sense of political reality. The conclusion to which this train of argument leads is a pervasive scepticism as to the possibility of any form of moral judgment on institutions and policies that is more than a pseudo-universal expression of limited and selfish interests.

It would seem to follow from this view of moral judgment that it must play a sharply reduced role in history, since the realities with which the historian has to deal are after all the interests of the various contending parties and not the ideal, moralizing formulations in which these interests are clothed. And it would also appear that in the absence of moral criteria that can claim any general validity, the historian must simply accept the testimony of events as to the superior efficacy or power of one society or system or policy over another without qualifying this judgment by events through any reflections of his own as to what alternative outcome might have been desirable on moral grounds. This is in fact very close to the position Carr develops in *What Is History?*; and the conception of historical progress he proposes there seems to dispense entirely with criteria of a recognizably moral kind. There are references to a "sense of direction in history which alone enables us to order and interpret the events of the past . . . and to liberate and organize human energies in the present with a view to the future," but Carr also tells us that "only the future can provide the key to the interpretation of the past"; and that since "history . . . is a record of what people did, not of what they failed to do, to this extent it is inevitably a success story."[8] It follows that the historian must necessarily concern himself principally with the forces that triumph and not with those that are defeated, and in his account of the Russian Revolution and of the construction of the Soviet state Carr has conformed to his own prescription. He wastes very little time or sympathy on the "might-have-beens," and appears at every step to accept the inevitability of the course that was in fact taken. What is puzzling, however, is his persistently adverse judgment of the alternative lines of policy that were represented by the bourgeois and Menshevik groups. It is not so much that one expects Carr to follow the defeated into exile or to compose eulogies for policies that did not prevail; but he could surely have left open questions about the value of the alternatives they represented instead of inferring that they must have been untenable from the fact that they did not prevail, as he often appears to do. In general, Carr's retrospective endorsement of Bolshevik policies does not seem to express any deep personal sympathy with their cause so much as it does a pervasive moral scepticism that makes any directly moral evaluation of events inadmissible. When such a scepticism is coupled with a belief that history is in some sense progressive, it is not just moral judgments as such that disappear from the historical record but a sense of multiple alternative possibilities as well. One can agree with Carr that there is something tiresome about the compulsion so many historians have felt to award good and bad moral marks to their subjects and yet one can still feel that such overtly judgmental attitudes are preferable to one which like his own, accepts only the authority of events and rests finally on scepticism.

In rejecting historical judgments that appeal to supra-historical standards of good and evil, Carr's conception of history reveals a surprising degree of affinity with ideas developed in the quite different tradition of national history, especially among German historians and philosophers of history. In my first chapter, I have already had occasion to take note of a conception of the historical enterprise worked out in nineteenth-century Germany on the basis of a critique of the older Natural Law theory of the state in which the controlling ethical assumptions of West-

---

[8]*What Is History?* (New York: Knopf, 1961), pp. 161, 167.

ern social thought had received their definitive philosophical statement. This movement of thought, which was closely associated with philosophical idealism and thus with the Hegelian system, came to be known as *historicism*. Like Hegel, though without his disposition to assume that the principal organizing structures of the historical process are derivable from a priori analyses, the historicists discerned the working out of a teleological pattern or, as they often expressed it, of an "idea" in the apparent chaos of historical experience. Again, like Hegel and the idealists generally, they believed that the nation-state constituted the most significant unit for the purposes of historical analysis. It was in fact something like the chosen instrument of the historical process if not in fact, as Ranke had claimed, a "thought of God." But a history that takes the state as its focus of interest will be for the most part political and military history; it will, as nineteenth-century German historiography did, concern itself in the first instance with the lives and achievements of the leaders of the state—world historical figures like Bismarck or Napoleon, in whom the historical process in the Hegelian phrase gains a partial consciousness of its own direction. In the drama of history as it is portrayed by historians of this tendency, the nameless masses of humanity who fight the wars, till the crops, and die in epidemics remain nameless; and the evolution of technology, demographic movements, and the development of trade form, at most, part of the historical background against which the central actors move toward the fulfillment of the historical tasks that are theirs. Other than statesmen and generals, the only individuals who receive sustained attention are the thinkers and poets who express the self-understanding of their time. In them, too, the meaning of events is raised to the level of consciousness; and ideally their vision would both guide and interpret the efforts of those who exercise power.

There is a deep paradox inherent in this conception of historiography and in the practice of those historians who adopted it. It interprets human history as the progressive realization of the moral vocation of man and it regards the state as the essential framework within which the ethical life achieves concreteness and reality. This would seem to be politico-moral history in its purest form; and the decisive influence that is attributed to the actions of a few individual men might well be thought to require that the historian examine the lives and character of these men with a view to defining and assessing their moral quality and the consequences, in moral terms, of the actions they performed. But this is not in fact what happened. The assumption that the state was an ethical entity influenced most German historians of the late nineteenth and early twentieth century in quite a different way. Instead of stimulating the kind of ethical appraisal to which one would have thought the state as an ethical entity must be subject, it operated as a guarantee that the state and its leaders were proof against ethically motivated criticism, since the latter would typically take the form of an application to these exceptional beings of standards that have their place only in private and domestic life. Thus, an action which in a private individual would constitute an unconscionable breach of faith or even a crime was assessed by quite different criteria when it was the act of a statesman. The latter thus benefited from the double assurance that his actions were, in a higher sense, ethically justified and—since that sense was never defined in a way that would entail specific restrictions—that he might do pretty much as he pleased. There have, of course, been complicated attempts to justify this system of double moral bookkeeping, but they have not made clear how the ethical vocation of the state can be separated from its vulnerability to ethically motivated criticism without seriously undercutting one or the other. In any case, one may suspect that the viability of the whole enterprise was heavily dependent on the success—as judged by other than moral standards—of the political ventures for which these historians were in some sense making themselves the moral underwriters. It was not until the final disaster that overtook the German state in 1945 that there was widespread reappraisal of the assumptions German historians had made about the moral role of the state. In fairness, it should be added that while the hazards of an a priori predisposition toward a positive ethical estimate of the activities of the national state are most obvious in the case of the German historians of the nineteenth and twentieth centuries, they are present in the historiographical practice of other nations as well. The Germans had explicitly formulated the theory that supported such positive evaluations; and therefore the experience of a profoundly unethical and even criminal state invalidated the postulates on which their historiographical practice rested in an uniquely direct way. But the theory they had thus formulated was one which historians of other countries have often followed implicitly, and therefore the lesson to be drawn from the evolution of German historiography in our century is one of wide relevance.

That evolution can be followed clearly in the career and writings of Friedrich Meinecke, whom many would regard as the premier German historian of the first half of the twentieth century. In the early work which made his reputation, *Weltbürgertum und Nationalstaat* (1908), Meinecke gave a brilliant account of the movements of thought which, from the late eighteenth century onward, were associated with the creation of a unified German state.[9] The key concepts in his analysis were

---

[9]This work has been translated by R. J. Kimber as *Cosmopolitanism and the National State* (Princeton, N.J.: Princeton University Press, 1970). *Die Idee der Staatsraison* has been translated by D. Scott as *Macchiavellianism* (New Haven: Yale University Press, 1957).

those of culture and power and of the relationship between them. Meinecke showed how thinkers like Wilhelm von Humboldt in the last decades of the eighteenth century had worked out a conception of *Bildung* or culture as the realization of the creative potentialities of the individual human being. This interpretation of culture was virtually apolitical, since all functions of growth and creativity were assigned to individuals and the state was confined to the negative or morally neutral task of maintaining the minimum of security and public order in which such individuals would be able to realize the promise that lay within them. Meinecke then went on to demonstrate how these essentially nonpolitical philosophers of culture progressively came to take a more favorable view of the positive ethical mission of the state. This evolution in the attitudes of thinkers like Humboldt, which was of course closely connected with the German national renaissance during the Napoleonic Wars, was one which Meinecke viewed with unmistakable approval. It was a movement away from a culture of the inner life, which is always threatened with sterility and preciosity, toward one that requires that personal idealism find its ultimate expression in public deeds and in the creation of appropriate institutional forms. Meinecke belonged to a generation which believed that in the German national state that came into being in 1870, the cultural ideals of the period of Goethe and Humboldt had achieved a large measure of realization and that culture and power had been fruitfully associated with one another under its auspices.

The rest of Meinecke's career is the story of his slow and reluctant movement away from this belief in the successful synthesis of culture and power in the institutions and policies of Imperial Germany. The story is the more interesting since Meinecke had extensive personal connections with political and military figures of the time and even played a certain advisory role in the politics of his day. The First World War was the turning point in Meinecke's development, although it began with a great surge of national feeling in which all classes—even the Socialists, as he approvingly notes—shared. But the question of war aims created deep divisions within the German political world and Meinecke, who had felt some anxieties because of the violation of Belgium's neutrality, was unable to espouse the expansionist aims of the German Right. As a self-described "conservative reformer," he worked for the remainder of the war and thereafter for a politics of reconciliation—a reconciliation of classes within Germany and a reconciliation of Germany with her European neighbors. His views, of course, did not prevail; but the experience of finding himself in opposition led him to reevaluate the ideas of the moral character of the state whose development he had followed in his earlier work. In *Die Idee der Staatsraison* (1924) he recognizes openly that the attribution of a moral vocation to the national state in the manner of Hegel and Ranke lends itself to perverted and amoral use in the hands of statesmen who are less prudent than a Bismarck or less scrupulous than a Stein. He still found a dualistic interpretation of the relationship of ethics and politics along the old Natural Law lines unacceptable, however, and he appealed instead for a return to the original Goethean conception of creative individuality in which the ethical is harmoniously related to the total self-realization of a human being without being reduced to the status of an ideological pretext for an amoral will to power. He was to make this appeal again, after the Second World War and the collapse of the Hitler regime, which had forced his retirement. For Meinecke, as for many other cultivated Germans of his time, the ideals of the *Goethezeit* had become a kind of comprehensive aesthetic-cum-ethical philosophy of the good life. They had, as Meinecke recognized, been traduced by that effort to translate them into public and institutional life which he had earlier viewed with so much hope. But to return to them in their pure original form was to return to the attempt to make a philosophy of personal self-realization yield a public ethic; and Meinecke never made clear how the "Goethe communities," for whose formation he called in the post-war period, would resolve this duality.

During the years when Meinecke was revising his earlier views of the moral quality of the state, other historians, mostly in France, were moving away from the politico-moral historiography that centers on states and statesmen, for quite different reasons. The ethical function of historiography has typically been exercised through an interpretation and critique of the motives and consequences of human action and, more particularly, of the actions of those men who are in positions of political and military leadership. As I have already noted, these actions have also been supposed to guide the movement of history toward some ideal fulfillment; together they constitute the dramatic sequences of events that have been called "l'histoire événementielle." One of the main reasons historians in this century have moved away from politico-moral history in the old style is that they have come to feel doubts about "l'histoire événementielle" on at least two major counts. First it has come to seem highly questionable whether the world historical figures with which politico-moral history typically concerned itself in fact enjoy the kind of freedom in relation to the social and economic infrastructure that is implied in the claim that they are the agents of a higher historical mission that must be understood in ethical terms. It has been suggested by Raymond Aron that the very simplicity of the structure of events in the ancient world made the dramatic and moral interpretation of great occurrences like the Peloponnesian War appropriate.[10] In the modern

---

[10]Raymond Aron, "Thucydide et le récit des événements," *History and Theory*, Vol. I (1962), 103–28.

world, especially, it is argued, both the complexity of events and the number of protagonists are so much greater than in the ancient world that the very possibility of focusing one's account on the character and actions of a few leading figures has become problematic. The latter thus come to seem less the imperious shapers of their nations' and the world's destiny and more the temporary representatives of larger historical forces which they can neither fully rationalize nor control. These forces are, at bottom, simply the coercive pressures exercised upon statesmen by the implicit requirements of the society they "lead"—i.e., by the expectations and demands that go with the permanent routines of life of those persons and groups whose interests they represent. These routines are themselves made up of purposeful human actions, whether they be procreation or steel manufacture; but they are typically not reflective in character and they are performed without anyone's having a clear sense of what their cumulative effect will be, much less the power to control it. They are, therefore, in a clear sense less eligible for appraisal in ethical terms, since it really does not make much sense to ask whether or not a Chinese peasant is acting rightly when he adds another child to his family. But if the "leaders" who may have some understanding of the demographic consequences of that action are very narrowly circumscribed in what they can do to forestall them, then their actions will come to seem just as compulsory and just as unsuited to ethical appraisal as are the actions of those who do not have their perspective on events. Their policies will, on this interpretation, be largely *commanded* by events rather than by any act of will or choice that is based on a principled attitude or that seeks to revise the course of events projected by these "routines of life"—rather than simply serving them. It follows that an historian's account of what a statesman so circumstanced does is not likely to concentrate on his situation as a moral being who has to determine in some measure the direction of events, for this interpretation of his possibilities is assumed to be in large measure an illusion. Instead, it will focus on those aspects of his activity that are not peculiar to him as an individual but are believed to be such as almost anyone in his position would exhibit. In this way, and by this logic, world historical figures and their actions come to share in the same anonymity the older historiographical tradition had assigned to the masses they were supposed to lead.

The other consideration that has influenced the reservations many historians now feel about "l'histoire événementielle" is of a different order. It has to do with the discovery that areas of human life which had been neglected by politico-moral history and even regarded as being in principle non-historical because they had to do with the material conditions of life rather than with the higher life of volition, have a history of their own that is of absorbing interest. The claims of economic history have been recognized, if not always honored in practice, for some time, but more recently the historical study of population movements—demographic history—has emerged, as have the history of technology, agricultural history—the study of the way men have used the earth for human purposes—and generally the study of the geographical setting of human activity. In a real sense it is now often argued, a region, a river, or a sea may be as much the central protagonist of a history as the human leaders of the societies that inhabit them; and it is surely significant that the title of the book that is often regarded as the masterpiece in this genre—Fernand Braudel's *La Méditerranée et le monde méditerranéen dans l'âge de Phillipe II*—gives pride of place to the name of the sea, not to that of the king.[11] The intent of historical work along these lines is not really to exclude political history, but to do a much fuller justice to the whole range of human life than was ever possible in a narrowly politico-moral history; in Braudel's book the detailed description of the Mediterranean world is followed by brilliant portraits of figures like Philip II and Don John of Austria and an equally striking account of the principal political and military events of the time which draws much of its persuasiveness from the sense of setting and circumstances which had been built up earlier. But the general tendency of such historiography, even in its most masterly exemplifications, is clearly not to emphasize the ethico-political "moment" but rather to incorporate the lives of all—statesmen and laborers, generals and children—into the rhythms of a world that evolves very slowly and then for the most part not in response to political and ethical initiatives. In the exploration of this broadened historical world, historians have increasingly drawn on the resources and methods of other disciplines, notably those of the social sciences: statistics, econometrics, anthropolgy, and geography. Since these disciplines are not primarily concerned with human beings in their capacity as moral agents, it is not surprising that the use of their methods of analysis has tended to move history still farther from the politico-moral style of its past.

It would, however, be a mistake to assume that these new approaches to history can make no contribution at all to a humanistic—and thus at least indirectly moral—interest in the past. By illuminating the condition of life of the great anonymous bulk of humanity, as that condition is reflected in price indices, mortality rates, or school curricula, such histories invite a new assessment of societies which we may have known until now almost entirely through the medium of the "high culture" of a tiny and privileged minority. It is not surprising either that this new

---

11Fernand Braudel, La Méditerranée et le monde méditerranéen dans l'âge de Philippe II (Paris: Colin, 1949).

knowledge of how the great mass of people lived should have stimulated a positive sympathy on the part of many historians for the under-class in the societies they study and especially for such impoverished and oppressed classes as, for example, the slave populations of Brazil and the United States in the nineteenth century, which had scarcely been recognized as having a history at all. Although this attitude is especially common among historians who are disillusioned with the liberal tradition of historiography and have turned in many cases to Marxism as an alternative framework of interpretation, it may also be regarded as effecting a downward translation of the moral interest of the older liberalism in the progress of freedom, to classes which liberal history could never really bring itself to include in its politico-moral history in any very meaningful way. Many historical episodes which involved the action of the masses and which were treated by liberal historians as simply cases of banditry or riot have recently been set in an altogether different moral perspective by historians who discern in them primitive expressions of political intent on the part of groups without representation in the formal political system. Again, in the work of the English historian E. P. Thompson, notably *The Formation of the English Working Class*, one finds a brilliant example of a strongly partisan and moral history in which the historian endorses the cause of his protagonist, the working class, as unambiguously as any liberal historian ever did that of Hampden and Pym.[12] Even more interesting from the moralist's point of view is the work that has been done on the history of slavery, especially in the United States. Here one finds a portrayal of the Negro experience of slavery by Kenneth Stampp which is dominated by a strong sense of the intolerable moral evil that slavery represents.[13] In *The Peculiar Institution* he argues that the experience of the black slave was in its essentials that of any person who is kidnapped, imprisoned, and made the chattel of another man; and one senses that this interpretation of the slave's experience of his condition is guided as much by the author's moral judgment on slavery as it is by the actual testimony of the slaves. Against this view, there is the argument of Stanley Elkins, which draws on psychological studies of the behavior of human beings in extreme situations like concentration camps, and suggests that in the analogous situation of enslavement, personality structure accommodates itself to what would otherwise be an absolutely hopeless and intolerable situa-

---

[12]E. P. Thompson, *The Making of the English Working Class* (New York: Pantheon Books, 1963).

[13]Kenneth Stampp, *The Peculiar Institution: Slavery in the Ante-Bellum South* (New York: Knopf, 1956).

tion.[14] The accommodation takes the form of a childlike and passive acceptance of the role that is assigned by the master; where it is complete, the possibility of an independent and adverse judgment on the fate which has been forced on one is virtually excluded. It would be wrong to read into these views an apologia for slavery as some have done. If this interpretation is correct, it only further substantiates the moral wrong that slavery entails when it makes self-disqualification as a moral agent a condition of survival. At the same time, such a conception of the slave's understanding of his own condition does complicate the task of those historians who still tend to impute to the oppressed of all times and places a community of consciousness and purpose that springs from their understanding of their true condition and their inner rejection of it.

Ethical interest of a different kind attaches to the recent development of "psycho-history," which draws on the resources of psychology and psychoanalytic theory to illuminate dimensions of historical experience which have been almost completely neglected. The effort to bring psychoanalytical insights to bear upon the interpretation of historical events began with Freud himself who, in his later years, extended his interests into a kind of speculative prehistory of man and also attempted to analyze the personality of a contemporary statesman, Woodrow Wilson, in the light of his own theory.[15] More recently, the effort to interpret the historical process in psychodynamic terms has assumed many different forms—some highly speculative and prophetic, like the work of N. O. Brown and others, more empirical and limited in scope, like the studies of R. J. Lifton.[16] Running through this literature is a strong sense of the negative and repressive character of ethical consciousness in its most familiar forms and an equally strong remedial intention that looks to an eventual liberation from the suffering and self-mutilation that are entailed by the present organization of our psychic economies. In the work of Erik Erikson in particular, this ethical element in psycho-historical work is very clearly in evidence; and in major studies he has applied his conceptions of ego-strengths and the identity crisis that accompany their acquisition to the interpretation of the lives of two men, Mahatma Gandhi and Martin Luther, who played roles of great importance in

---

[14]Stanley Elkins, *Slavery: A Problem in American Institutional and Intellectual Life* (Chicago: University of Chicago Press, 1959).

[15]Sigmund Freud and William C. Bullitt, *Thomas Woodrow Wilson: A Psychological Study* (Boston: Houghton Mifflin, 1967).

[16]N. O. Brown, *Life Against Death: The Psychoanalytic Meaning of History* (Middletown, Conn.: Wesleyan University Press, 1959); R. J. Lifton, *Death In Life: Survivors of Hiroshima* (New York: Random House, 1967) and *History and Human Survival* (New York: Random House, 1970).

modern history.[17] In both cases his effort is to understand how a Luther and a Gandhi were capable, in a psychodynamic sense, of the achievements which gave them their place in history—achievements which in both cases had a strongly ethical character. In the one, it was the enunciation and institutionalization of a drastically modified conception of the man-God relationship and thus of man's moral capacities and responsibilities; and in the other, the development of a creed and practice of nonviolent resistance which was to animate the movement for the liberation of India from British rule. The question Erikson asks is *how* these accomplishments became psychologically possible for these individual human beings in the circumstances in which they found themselves. In both cases, the answer he gives involves an isomorphism between relationships within the personal life of the man in question—Luther's relationship to his father, Gandhi's to both his parents—and their larger relationships—to God or to India; and both Luther and Gandhi are portrayed as reenacting on the larger stage of history a role that was prefigured in their personal intrafamilial life. Perhaps even more important, however, is the way Erikson characterizes the problem that Gandhi tried to solve through *satyagraha* in terms that identify it as an evolutionary crisis for man as a species which must control its use of violence if it is to survive. *Gandhi's Truth* is written out of the conviction that opposition to injustice too often follows a psychological strategy which in the end produces even greater hatred and violence; and in Gandhi's life Erikson sees the promise of a way out of the impasse in which men find themselves. An historical biography of this kind clearly conceives its subject in ethical terms and is itself an ethical act, since it is an effort to make the hope for man that Gandhi's life contains more generally understood.

II

In my discussion of history I have tried to show how doubts about the validity of the various moral perspectives that have been used for the interpretation of historical events have led to a more cautious and ambivalent use of them and in some cases to forms of historical inquiry in which they are ostensibly dispensed with altogether. The situation in respect to literature is somewhat different. There the commitment to a concern with individual human beings and with the meaning and worth of what they do and are is even deeper than it has traditionally been in

---

[17]Erik Erikson, *Young Man Luther* (New York: Norton, 1958) and *Gandhi's Truth* (New York: Norton, 1969).

Doubleday, 1968. An expository account and critique of positivistic philosophy.

LERNER, DANIEL, ed., *The Human Meaning of the Social Sciences.* New York: Meridian Books, 1959. Essays dealing with ethical aspects of the social sciences. The essays by Edward Shils and Clyde Kluckhohn are of special interest.

MEYERHOFF, HANS, ed., *The Philosophy of History in Our Time.* Garden City, New York: Doubleday, 1959. A good anthology which includes reflective essays on historical thought by a number of practising historians.

POLANYI, MICHAEL, *Beyond Nihilism.* Cambridge, England: Cambridge University Press, 1960. A diagnosis of the moral temper of our time by a scientist turned philosopher.

ROTENSTREICH, NATHAN, *Between Past and Present: An Essay on History.* New Haven, Connecticut: Yale University Press, 1958. A re-appraisal of the value and significance of historical study by a philosopher and humanist.

SARTRE, JEAN-PAUL, *What Is Literature,* trans. by Bernard Frechtman. New York: Washington Square Press, 1966. An existential account of writing (and reading) as an exercise of human freedom.

index

A

Acton, Lord, 92
Adorno, T. W., 65
Anouilh, Jean, 114
Aragon, Louis, 122–23
Arnold, Thurman, 44
Aron, Raymond, 101–2
Arrow, K. J., 54
Austin, John, 47

B

Barth, Karl, 36
Beard, Charles, 93–94

Beckett, Samuel, 113, 117–18
Benedict, Ruth, 67
Bentham, Jeremy, 47
Bonhoeffer, Dietrich, 36–37
Bradley, F. H., 5–6
Brandeis, Louis D., 43
Braudel, Fernand, 103
Brecht, Berchtold, 123
Brown, N. O., 105
Burnham, James, 49
Butterfield, Herbert, 92, 94

C

Camus, Albert, 37, 125–26

Carnap, Rudolph, 12–13, 14, 16
Carr, E. H., 95–97
Claudel, Paul, 119
Compton-Burnett, Ivy, 108
Comte, Auguste, 15
Conrad, Joseph, 107, 108, 123–24, 126
Croce, Benedetto, 8–9

D

Dahrendorf, Ralf, 61
Dewey, John, 20, 21, 22, 40
Durkheim, Emile, 39, 54–55

E

Eliot, George, 113
Eliot, T. S., 113–14
Elkins, Stanley, 104–5
Erikson, Erik, 77, 105–6

F

Forster, E. M., 13, 108, 109–10
Fox, Charles James, 92
Frank, Jerome, 44
Freud, Sigmund, 71–78, 105
Fromm, Eric, 77
Fuller, Lon, 46

G

Galbraith, J. K., 53
Gandhi, Mahatma, 105–6
Gide, Andre, 118, 119–20, 121
Goethe, J. W. von, 100, 101
Gramsci, Antonio, 12

H

Hand, Learned, 43
Hare, R. M., 34
Hart, H. L. A., 46–47
Hegel, G. W. F., 4, 8, 11, 18, 25, 32, 35, 98
Heidegger, Martin, 27, 29–30, 31, 32
Heller, Eric, 88
Hemingway, Ernest, 121
Hofstadter, Richard, 90–91, 93, 94, 95
Humboldt, Wilhelm von, 100
Husserl, Edmund, 26–27, 32

J

James, Henry, 107-8, 109, 110
James, William, 21
Jaspers, Karl, 33
Joyce, James, 113–15

K

Kafka, Franz, 113, 115–17
Kant, Immanuel, 4, 25, 31, 87
Kelsen, Hans, 44–45
Kennan, George, 42
Keynes, J. M., 51, 52–53
Kierkegaard, Soren, 32–33, 36
Kluckhohn, Clyde, 68
Koestler, Arthur, 124–25
Kolakowski, Leszek, 12

L

Lasswell, Harold, 49
Lawrence, D. H., 108, 110–11
Lawrence, T. E., 120
Leavis, F. R., 107–8
Lenin, V. I., 122

Levi-Strauss, Claude, 69
Lifton, R. J., 105
Lukacs, Gyorgy, 12
Luther, Martin, 92, 94, 105–6
Lynd, Robert, 60

M

Macaulay, Thomas B., 92
Machiavelli, Niccolo, 49
Mailer, Norman, 121
Malinowski, Bronislaw, 67
Malraux, Andre, 118, 119, 120–21
Mann, Thomas, 73, 109
Mannheim, Karl, 48
Marcel, Gabriel, 33
Marcuse, Herbert, 65
Marx, Karl, 9, 10, 11, 12, 33, 47, 58–59
Mauriac, François, 121
McDougall, William, 70
Meinecke, Friedrich, 99–101
Merleau-Ponty, Maurice, 12, 35
Merton, Robert, 68
Moore, G. E., 13–14, 22, 26
Morgenthau, Hans, 42
Mosca, Gaetano, 49
Myrdal, Gunnar, 60

N

Neurath, Otto, 17
Niebuhr, Reinhold, 36, 42
Nietzsche, Friedrich, 28, 29, 47, 88, 118

O

O'Hara, John, 109
Orwell, George, 124, 125

P

Pareto, Vilfredo, 54, 57
Parrington, V. L., 93
Parsons, Talcott, 54, 62–63
Piaget, Jean, 71, 82–84
Plato, 2, 13, 18, 26
Popper, Karl, 17, 18, 60
Proust, Marcel, 109

R

Radbruch, Gustav, 46
Ranke, Leopold von, 98
Rieff, Philip, 74–75
Riesman, David, 76
Royce, Josiah, 5
Russell, Bertrand, 22, 26

S

Sartre, Jean-Paul, 30, 31–32, 87, 121
Scheler, Max, 26, 27
Schlesinger, Jr., A.M., 94
Schlick, Moritz, 17
Schwartz, Delmore, 109
Silone, Ignazio, 124, 125
Skinner, B. J., 79–82
Smith, Adam, 51
Sorel, Georges, 48
Spinoza, Benedict, 2, 49
Stampp, Kenneth, 104
Stevenson, Charles L., 18, 19, 20

T

Thompson, E. P., 104
Trilling, Lionel, 107, 113
Turner, F. J., 93, 94

V

Veblen, Thorstein, 40, 53

W

Weber, Max, 39, 54–58, 59, 61, 63

Westermarck, E. A., 66
Wharton, Edith, 109
White, Morton, 39–40
Wilson, Woodrow, 42, 105
Wittgenstein, Ludwig, 1, 14, 22, 23, 24–25, 34, 35
Woolf, Virginia, 13, 111–12